Initial praise for Fifty Latin Da

Youlie Mouzafiarova has accomplished an interesting and challenging task in writing this book, giving amateur and professional dancers and dance teachers a valuable collection of exercises for the Latin American dances to increase their performance skills and teaching methods.

Through her professional experience as a dancer and teacher and having an individual and insightful mind into the different aspects of dance technique, Youlie presents helpful and useful advice throughout her book.

I'm sure having this structured written approach, adding to the growing knowledge of dance, will help find a new facet to the serious scientific approach to dance and consequently deliver greatly improved dancing. I wish the author and her book a welldeserved success!

Leonid Pletnev, Moscow, Russia
Honorary President of the International Dance Union (IDU)
President of Dance System "Reverence" (Russia)
Worldwide famous coach and adjudicator
Author of book *With Reverence. About life in dancing and dancing in life*

Congratulations to Youlie for producing an excellent and long awaited system of well-defined exercises that can only enhance all the various Latin dances being performed in today's world. The content is extremely precise and put together with so much thought for each Individual dance.

Applied correctly, following Youlie's methods with consistent practice, can only lead to having an improved performance creating exquisite body and leg lines, actions and angles, thus creating those beautiful pictures in movement we all strive for. It is with pleasure to highly recommend this book from a truly great artist, teacher and friend in the modern world of Latin American dances and rhythms.

Keith Kelly, London, UK
Fellow & Examiner IDTA

Congratulations to Youlie Mouzafiarova for her efforts to create a book with fundamental Latin dance exercises which I consider very necessary and missing on the dance market. Undoubtedly it will help every dancer, teacher and coach who is aiming to master their craft for executing, recognizing, analyzing and transfering the real assets of this style of dancing. The late great Walter Laird put some ideas about it on paper years ago, but unfortunately it wasn't developed any further. Now we have on hand a wonderful instrument for perfecting our personal expression in Latin dance through practice of postural principles and deeper understanding of the "Actions used" in every part of our brilliant human bodies for every single beat of every bar in the music – a difficult task, but a marvellous challenge. Good luck fellows and well done Youlie!

Zlatin Kostov, Sofia, Bulgaria
Fellow IDTA
Ass. Prof. on Dancesport training NSA

I found Youlie's pages of basic information for poise and style extremely useful for exercises, dancing and even in competition.

Daniel YK Yan, Hong Kong
Fellow and Examiner IDTA

I endorse this book of Latin dance exercises by Youlie Mouzafiorava as being helpful to all dancers of the world, in timing, in flexibility, in power, in grace and to keep them strong and live longer.

Socrates A Charos, Florida, USA
Producer of dance shows 'The World of Dance' and of the first Dance Olympiade in modern times in Athens, Greece

Every experienced teacher will know that there are many times a Latin dancer will ask the question, 'What do I do with my arms?' With the suggested arm exercises clearly given by, Youlie, plus with the help of the finished arm positions in the photographs, this query will soon be heard less and less in your class lessons. Arm exercises are just part of the 50 Latin Exercises to be found in this book.

Ken Akrill, Hull, UK
Fellow & Examiner UKA
Former Triple Examiner IDTA (Retired)
Author of *UKA Ballroom & Latin Technique*

Fifty Latin Dance Exercises

Youlie Mouzafiarova

with David Pullinger

To Susanna
from Youlie with
best wishes & lots of love!
Keep dancing!
26.07.12
London.

FastPrint Publishing

First published 2012 by Fast-Print Publishing
of Peterborough, England.
www.fast-print.net/store.php

1st Edition May 2012
2nd Edition June 2012

Fifty Latin Dance Exercises

www.youliedance.com
youlie@atticadance.com

ISBN: 978-178035-392-0

A catalogue record for this book is available from the British Library

Photographs and cover photograph: Dimitra Vavanellou
www.photostudioada.com

Text and cover design: Lisa Kirkham

Shoes by Grand Prix: www.allfordance.com

An environmentally friendly book printed and bound in England by
www.printondemand-worldwide.com

Mixed Sources
Product group from well-managed forests, and other controlled sources
www.fsc.org Cert no. TT-COC-002641
© 1996 Forest Stewardship Council
FSC

PEFC Certified
This product is from sustainably managed forests and controlled sources
www.pefc.org
PEFC
PEFC/16-33-415

This book is made entirely of chain-of-custody materials

Dedicated to my Father
ANATOLIY MOUZAFIAROV
1950–2005

A great encourager and teacher
of what is of real value in life

YOULIE MOUZAFIAROVA

Dancer, Choreographer, Coach
and International Adjudicator

Fellow and Examiner IDTA

General Secretary of Greek Dance Sport Association

Former 10 Dance Champion of Kazakhstan and Greece

Former Latin Balkan Champion

Former Ballroom Showcase Greek Champion

David Pullinger is a dance student and writer.

Preface

I'm passionate about dancing and helping people to dance well. As a dancer, coach, examiner and adjudicator, it gives me pleasure to see couples moving naturally and expressing the distinctive essence of each of the different Latin dances.

Most kinds of dance use preparatory exercises as a means of stretching and strengthening the required muscle groups, coordinating their use, developing control, and as warm-up each and every time when about to dance. This is important in preventing injury and increases the capacity of muscles to perform and so is helpful for dancers of all abilities and experience. That's why I developed these exercises for the Latin dances.

The exercises are the result of many years experience in dancing and coaching amateurs and professionals. I've seen excellent results from their use, with improved quality of movement providing an effective foundation for more complex figures and choreographies. Breaking figures down into basic physical movements and repeating them is helpful to condition bodies for dance and make movements more natural.

Over the past twenty years, the understanding of bodily movement in Latin dance has developed rapidly and, in particular, the integration of the core in the middle part of the body with the other main muscle groups has helped create a more flowing, strong, rhythmic and sensual movement. As a result, the overall effect is one of stronger integration and precision, leading to better shaping and longer body lines.

Although most of the exercises are intended for personal work, individually or with a teacher, I have included a group of partner exercises in order to develop connection, without which dance cannot be led or followed. Many rightly learn their parts of a dance, but there also needs to be the correct connection that brings two partners into a dynamic interaction.

One of my main aims is to provide a set of exercises that bring out the unique features and characteristics of each Latin dance. By building these in at the foundation through the basic movements, the distinctive look and feel of each dance is more naturally expressed.

I share these exercises with a hope that many people will look and feel better in their dancing and, if they want to, compete with greater confidence and flair.

I wish to express my sincere gratitude to many people who have helped me over the years. My family has supported me in all aspects of my dance career, particularly my lovely mother, Sofia Pavlidi, and my brother, Yuri Mouzafiarov. I'm very fortunate to have had many wonderful teachers and mentors who shared their knowledge and experience with me, to each of them I express my sincere gratitude. Dance takes two people and my dance partner Alex Khoroshikh shared with me the journey of professional dancing and teaching for the past decade. I am also indebted to the opportunities presented by the International Dance Teachers Association (IDTA), with whom I have worked over many years and become a Fellow and Examiner. Through IDTA I have introduced these exercises to other IDTA teachers and students as a lecturer at the 2010 and 2011 Southport Annual Congresses and they were enthusiastic about their value and encouraged me to write them up for wider circulation.

In preparing this book, I want to acknowledge Dimitra Vavanellou for taking the photographs, Alex Khoroshikh for posing and Giota Malamou for editorial support. And, of course, thanks to all those students with whom I have worked developing these exercises and learnt how to use them for maximum effectiveness.

Youlie Mouzafiarova

London, April 2012

Contents

Definitions

Axis The imaginary line about which a body can rotate, being a vertical line from centre of gravity of the body to the point of contact on the floor, when the body is in any balanced position.

Balance In Latin dances, an even distribution of one's weight around the axis of the body over the foot or feet when stationary or moving.

Bounce action To move up and down in a spring-like manner using feet, ankles and knees. Slight bounce action is often used in progressive movements as a result of longer steps.

Chassé A combination of three steps in any direction, usually in two beats of music, the second step being closed or nearly together (half closed).

Check Often used as short form for Checked (or Last) Forward Walk on either foot, in which there is only part weight transfer onto the moving foot in order to brake the movement and change direction.

Compression Bending the knee with controlled pressing into the floor as preparation for releasing energy through straightening.

Flex Bending of a joint with slight tension, usually after straightening (for example the knee of the back leg in Last Forward Walk), when the foot remains in the same position.

Hip action Controlled rotation of the hips from right diagonal backward to left diagonal backward passing through a neutral position with hips level to the floor and conversely.

Isolation rotations Turns of individual parts of the body which are done independently.

Locked knee A knee that is straightened very well (sometimes called hyperextension, although care must be taken not to overdo this and cause long-term injury).

Pelvis action Movement of the pelvis tilting forwards or diagonally backwards.

Poise is the bearing and deportment of the body in the state of balance and equilibrium used for dancing. The different Latin dances have different poises because of their character, speed and rhythm.

Rotation A turning movement of the whole or parts of the body around an axis.

Rock action The Last Backward Step in Jive, with or without turn, using part weight transfer.

Settling The controlled relaxation of the hip joint while transferring weight gradually onto a leg with locked knee, allowing the hips to move slightly to the side and usually to rotate diagonally backwards so that, on completion, weight is felt to be near heel of foot. (The hip movement is diagonally forwards only for inward rotations and in some Backward Walks.)

Slip Foot slip resulting from pelvis or hip action and part weight transfer (for example in Samba Walks and in Cha cha cha Slip Close Chassé).

Spotting Keeping the head and eyes still and focused on one spot at eye level while the rest of the body rotates underneath followed by a sharp head rotation to the final direction before the body completes its turn.

Sway Inclination of the body to R or L from the feet to the top of the head.

Swing action Pendulum movement of the whole or individual parts of the body.

Twist Rotation of one or both feet when flat, usually as a result of body or hip rotation or both.

General notes

Abbreviations

Abbreviations are largely avoided in descriptions of the exercises. Although dancers would be expected to develop familiarity with standard abbreviations, the book is intended and useful for all levels. That is the reason for including only R and L for right and left and RF and LF for right and left feet.

Counts, Timing and Beat Values

These exercises are designed for improving technique, conditioning and warm-up. Some Counts are chosen to show stages of the movement that are not always in the same timing as the dance. Advanced dancers may choose to alter timings and beat values to suit those used in figures.

Most dance movements are continuous. Describing them in language requires sequential description for movements that sometimes occur at the same time or continue throughout the Count.

Directions

At some points, instructions in exercises are described for clarity as if starting by facing a wall or mirror (except for the Connection exercises). All of them could, of course, be done in any direction suitable.

Figure Names

The names of dances and figures are as used in the IDTA Professional and Amateur Dance Syllabus 2010.

Hips and Pelvis

In this book , the word pelvis is used when there is forward tilt present and the word hips when there controlled rotation of the hips from right diagonal backwards to left diagonal backwards and vice-versa.

Latin

Throughout Latin dance is used as the the colloquial shorter version for Latin-American dance.

Photographs

The photographs show main stages, but not all, of the movement of the exercise; descriptions should also be read.

Editorial note:

The book uses British English spelling and punctuation. Forward and backward are used when adjectives or directions; forwards and backwards when adverbs describing movement. This also applies to inward, outward, upward and downward.

About these exercises

These exercises deal with actions and movements that are parts of Latin dance figures. They are intended to develop the basic constituent parts of dance movement for both leaders and followers. At every level – social and competitor – dance is made up of the basic technique of its components. Use of these exercises ensures that the foundations of each dance are solid. Dancers at all abilities and experience will find value in coming back to them time and again.

As an analogy, one might think of an exercise as a word, a figure as a sentence and a routine as a whole paragraph, with the choreography telling the story. Learning the actions and movements in these exercises will allow greater fluency of expression and more confidence in combining figures to tell a story.

Why use these exercises

Warm-up
Most kinds of dance have specific warm-up exercises to prepare the body for exercise and protect it from injury. These exercises deliver the specificity needed for Latin dance.

Develop muscle memory through repetition
The ability to perform the correct movement at the right time is key to dance. These exercises build the muscle memory required and make learning more advanced figures easier.

Get biomechanics working properly
Getting the correct skeletal-muscular patterns working is the secret to natural and strong movement. These building-block exercises are designed to do that.

Improve technique
Although Latin dances share some basic actions and movements, there are also specific ones particular to each Latin dance. For each Latin dance there are exercises to get the body moving correctly and differently.

Present great body lines
Body lines are created from stretching and extending muscles with correct biomechanics. Dancers can develop these by toning their muscles and extending their limits by regularly using these exercises.

When and where to use these exercises

Before a private or group class or practice
Dancers of all levels need to prepare their bodies for the correct movements in the dance being studied. Bodies can take time getting into dance mode, especially coming straight from home or place of study or work. General warm-up is useful, but it is not enough to develop the particular patterns of movement needed. Using the appropriate exercise as preparation is a valuable use of time and allows a better focus on later practice or learning of figures and routines.

For teachers, as main class or workshop
Sometimes exercises can be used by themselves in a workshop or technique class as a subject or theme for better technique. They help develop good habits and so enable new figures be learnt more effectively. This is particularly effective for mixed groups as the exercises are suitable and continue to be useful for every level of dancer.

At home, study or work
Use one or two exercises in practice in the midst of everyday life. They condition the body and enable the movements to become much more natural. It will be important that the practice is correct and it is recommended that a teacher reviews them regularly. My students have reported using them as a short break from sitting at desks working on computers and when cleaning, cooking or waiting for public transport.

Addressing a particular problem identified during a lesson or class
When teaching a group, there can be a common aspect that students would benefit from working on. Slotting the appropriate exercise into a group class for five minutes can make all the difference to the appearance of the dancing and confidence in learning.

How to use these exercises

Read through the exercise carefully before use and look at the photos.
Start by checking the dancing poise, which is why it is mentioned at the start of each exercise. In particular:
- straighten spine upwards
- engage abdominal and back muscles to lengthen the back
- keep pelvis perpendicular to floor by engaging glutes (gluteus muscle group)
- lift rib cages upwards but not outwards
- keep shoulders down and back
- extend neck upwards, keeping chin line parallel to the floor
- look straight ahead.

Begin each exercise step by step without Counts, checking the position at each stage.
Practice exercise to Counts and music:
- first to Count, using either the one described or an alternative
- then to slow music with Counts, using a rhythm track if available and slowing it down or using it at half tempo by counting, for example, two beats of music for one Count
- then to strict tempo music with Counts
- finally to strict tempo music without Counts.

Practice exercises in blocks of 4 – 8 repetitions and combine with other relevant exercises to the dance or subject and move through them without break.

Focus on a different part of the body in turn, for example, on feet, knees, hips, pelvis, sides, core, shoulders, arms, head. This builds precision of movement and timing.

Notes

Playing music throughout Optionally play music for the relevant Latin dance in the background throughout in order to connect the the body's memory to the muscle groups used. Hearing the music will then pre-condition the body for correct movement and co-ordinate muscle groups with the rhythm of the dance.

Shoewear and clothing These exercises can be best done wearing Latin shoes. For a change try barefooted, with socks, or ballet shoes. Clothing should be worn that allows free movement of all parts of the body and which enables body lines to be easily seen in a mirror or by a teacher.

Warm-up exercises

Many of these exercises can be used for warm-up prior to individual or couple practice, class, workshop or doing other Exercises in this book. They need not take long and help prevent the body from injury as well as preparing the body for the kinds of movement that are to be made.

Although each person and couple will develop their own preferred preparation for dance, I recommend the following as a starting point.

General stretching, with which is good to begin as it elongates the muscles and starts to warm them up.

Depending on what is planned for practice or class, then select some exercises common to several and/or specific to a Latin dance.

Subjects common to several or all dances:

Balance: a general exercise good for all Latin dance

Exercise 4 Balance

Rotations: each of the four isolated rotations

Exercise 40 Head isolation
Exercise 41 Chest isolation
Exercise 42 Pelvis isolation
Exercise 43 Lower legs isolation

Arm movements

Exercise 34 Forward and Downward Arm Movement
Exercise 35 Upward and Forward Arm Movement
Exercise 36 Wrist circles

Specific to each Latin dance:

Rumba Exercise 6 Weight changes in place

Cha cha cha Exercise 10 Pelvis action
Exercise 11 Hip action

Samba Exercise 15 Bounce action
Exercise 16 Pelvis action

Jive Exercise 21 Side swing with foot collection
Exercise 23 Diagonal swing action with foot collection

Paso Doble Exercise 28 Poise
Exercise 30 Sur Place

General Exercises

This group of exercises prepares the body for the specific ones for each dance. It is useful for Latin dancers of all abilities and experience to be reminded of the relevant dancing poise, to maintain it while moving, to be aware of the placing of body weight, and to develop greater balance while stationary or during movement.

1

Before dancing or exercising, it is useful to get to know the feeling of using the muscles that support the skeletal frame in the poise used for Latin dancing. For many sat at a computer or engaged in other activities >

1a

General dancing poise

Stand with feet together, placed flat on the floor and almost parallel with weight equally distributed, and:

- straighten spine upwards
- engage abdominal and back muscles to lengthen the back
- keep pelvis perpendicular to floor by engaging glutes
- lift rib cage upwards but not outwards
- keep shoulders down and back
- extend neck, keeping chin line parallel to the floor
- look straight ahead.

Place R arm on diaphragm and L arm on the lower part of back with hand facing out to feel the above.

Repeat by relaxing and starting again.

1b

Poise for Samba and Jive

In Samba and Jive the knees are not locked and weight is kept towards balls of the feet, except for a few figures using different timing because of the beat values.

Start with the general dancing poise and then move weight slightly forwards towards balls of feet.

Keep arms on diaphragm and lower back to ensure the body remains straight as the body weight is moved forwards. Optionally extend arms to the side at shoulder level, slightly forward and flexed, with palms of the hands facing downward.

Repeat by returning to general poise and starting again.

> during the day, this is not naturally attained. There is need to build the muscle memory so that the relevant poise for each dance becomes familiar enough to be maintained easily.

1c

Poise for Rumba and Cha cha cha

In Rumba and Cha cha cha knees are often locked, weight transferred between the ball and heel of the foot.

Start with the general dancing poise and, maintaining the same body and head position, either take a step to the L or extend R leg to side on toe with some pressure on toe of RF, moving almost full weight onto LF.

Lock both knees.

Extend arms to the side at shoulder level, slightly forward and flexed, with palms of the hands facing downward.

Repeat on RF, by returning to general poise and taking step to R or extending L leg.

1d

Poise for Paso Doble

In Paso Doble the poise reflects the strong curved body line of bull-fighters and flamenco dancers.

Start with the general dancing poise and transfer weight towards the balls of feet.

Tilt the pelvis forwards, allowing knees to flex slightly, with the head retaining the same height. End with the body in a curved line from the balls of the feet to the crown of the head.

At the same time, move arms upwards and turn elbows to bring hands to front, keeping upper arms slightly retracted at shoulder level.

(Described in more detail in Ex.28.)

2

In Latin dance, movement is initiated by the core (mid-body between the hands in the photos) that is the centre of gravity of a solo dancer. The body axis, being a vertical line from centre of gravity to the point of >

Start in general poise with feet apart, weight equally distributed on both feet flat, with knees straight but not locked.

Place R palm on diaphragm and L palm on lower part of the back facing outward.

2a
Feel how the body axis is vertical and passes through the centre of the body.

2b
Transfer weight onto RF and allow the heel of LF to release, toe on inside edge with some pressure into the floor.

Keep both knees straight.

Feel how the body axis is vertical and passes through the the R side of the body.

> contact on the floor, therefore moves. Awareness of this movement will develop better balance for moving, stopping and changing direction, while being in time with the music.

2c

Transfer weight towards L until equally distributed on both feet flat.

Feel how the body axis is vertical and passes through the centre of the body.

Keep both knees straight with feet flat.

2d

Transfer weight onto LF and allow the heel of RF to release, toe on inside edge with some pressure into the floor.

Keep both knees straight.

Feel how the body axis is vertical and passes through the the L side of the body.

Keep the spine straight and pelvis parallel to the floor throughout.

Repeat exercise as required, varying speed from slow to fast using Counts 1 – 8, 1 – 4, or 1 & 2.

Optionally use any Latin music.

Repeat with feet together, ensuring that the inside edges of the feet are used throughout and spine stays completely straight without settling, sway or side extension.

General | Moving axis forwards and backwards

3

The purpose of this exercise is to feel how the forward and backward movement of the body axis is initiated by the core, causing weight transfer in the feet when the whole body moves as a whole, like a >

Start in general poise with feet together and parallel with weight equally distributed on the centre of both feet.

Place R arm on diaphragm and L on the lower part of the back.

3a
Feel how the body axis passes through the centre of the feet perpendicular to the floor and body line is vertical.

Keep both knees straight but not locked throughout.

3b
Transfer weight from the centre of the feet towards the balls of the feet and then to toes keeping feet flat (without releasing heels from the floor) so the body axis moves forward.

Feel how the body line is leaning forward in a single line.

Keep the spine straight moving the body forwards as a whole.

> plank, without any change in poise at the waist or in the upper body. The body line will lean and the body axis pass through different parts of the feet from the toes through to the heels of the feet.

3c

Return to starting position.

Feel how the body axis again passes through centre of feet and body line is vertical and perpendicular to the floor.

3d

Transfer weight from centre of feet to heels without releasing the toes from the floor so the body axis moves backwards.

Keep the spine straight.

Feel how the body line is leaning backward in a single line.

The degree to which the axis moves forwards and backwards must only be such that the poise of the body is not affected.

Repeat exercise as required, varying speed from slow to fast using Counts 1 – 8, 1 – 4 or 1 & 2.

Optionally use any Latin music.

4

This is a key exercise to help develop good balance. It begins by developing balance on one foot while moving the other foot, then continues using rise and fall on one foot with the other stationary. >

Start in the general poise described in Exercise 1 (and pictured above).

4a

Place hands on hips or extend arms to the side at shoulder level, slightly forward and flexed, with palms of the hands facing downward.

4b

Transfer full weight onto RF and towards ball.

Feel the axis passing through the R side of the body.

Lift L knee slightly with toe pointing downward and ankle in contact with standing leg.

Stand still.

Continue exercise changing the height of LF on the standing leg.

Optionally vary the position of the L leg, for example by extending forwards, sideways and backwards.

> For beginners it may be advisable to use a ballet barre, chair or partner's shoulder(s) or arm(s) at the side or front for support for this exercise.

4c

Continue on RF, keep LF in same position on the standing leg throughout this part of the exercise.

Slowly and gradually rise onto toe of RF through the ankle and knee of the standing leg.

4d

Slowly and gradually with control lower onto RF flat and compress knee.

In this part of the exercise ensure the spine remains vertical and straight.

Repeat exercise standing on LF.

Optionally use counts 1 – 4 or 1 – 8 or any Latin music.

Advanced dancers repeat with eyes closed.

Rumba Exercises

The Rumba is the slowest of all the Latin dances and has a beauty that lies in its continuous fluid movement contrasted with sharp turns. This requires good coordination and control, which this set of exercises is designed to develop.

The set focuses on the settling action, one of the most distinctive elements of Rumba (also used in Cha cha cha). Settling is the controlled relaxation of the hip joint while transfering weight gradually onto a leg with locked knee, allowing the hips to move slightly to the side and to rotate diagonally backwards so that, on completion, weight is felt to be near heel of foot of standing leg.

In addition, Cha cha cha Exercises 13 and 14 may also be used for Rumba and later sets of exercises for the Rotations, Arms and Combination further develop coordination, control and continuity of movement.

5

The purpose of this exercise is to practice the controlled settling action of the body and hips, to maintain balance, retain the same height, and to learn to feel – and see, if using a mirror – the difference between >

Start in Rumba poise, with feet together and almost full weight on LF with L knee locked.

5a

Lift R knee slightly with toe pointing downward and place ankle in contact with inside of standing leg at calf level.

For better balance, extend arms to the side at chest level, slightly forward and flexed, with palms of the hands facing downward.

The body axis should be felt passing through the L side of the body and weight towards the ball of the LF.

5b

On Count 1

Relax the hip joint with control to commence the hips moving slightly to L and rotating diagonally backwards.

Keep the knee of the L leg locked.

Keep the R knee in the same forward line, without any rotation inwards or outwards.

> settling and level hips parallel to wall and floor.For beginners it may be advisable to use a ballet barre, chair or partner's shoulder(s) or arm(s) at the side or front for support for this exercise.

5c

On Count 2

Continue to rotate hips further diagonally backwards.

Keep R knee on the same forward line, by moving it slightly forwards.

Feel how body weight appears to be near heel of LF and the body axis moves slightly backwards.

Also feel how the side abdominal muscles stretch as a result of the rotation of the hips.

5d

On Counts 3-4

Return to starting position gradually.

The hips should return to a position level with the floor (for which it is useful to be in front of a mirror in early stages or check by placing hands on hips at the same level).

Throughout the exercise, ensure that the position of the upper part of the body is not affected, the same height is maintained throughout and the spine kept straight. This is achieved by:

– stretching the spine upwards
– tightening the glutes
– keeping shoulders facing forward
– allowing the side abdominal muscles to stretch during settling.

Repeat several times on LF, then on RF, using Counts 1 – 4 or Rumba or Cha cha cha music.

6

Weight changes with feet together are used extensively in the Rumba, for example the third step of the Cucaracha, the follower's first step in Alemana or Hockey Stick, and first step of Alternative Basic Movement. >

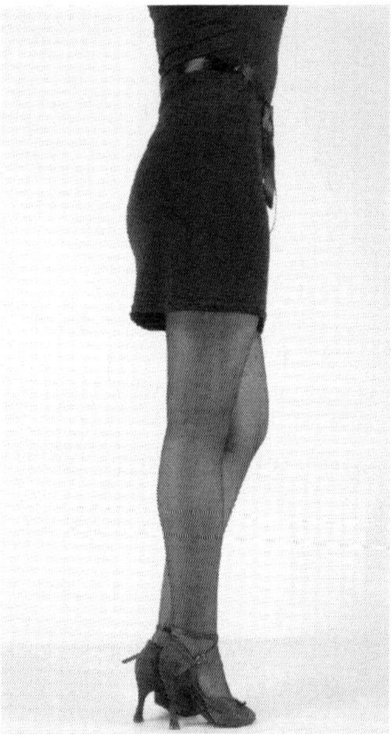

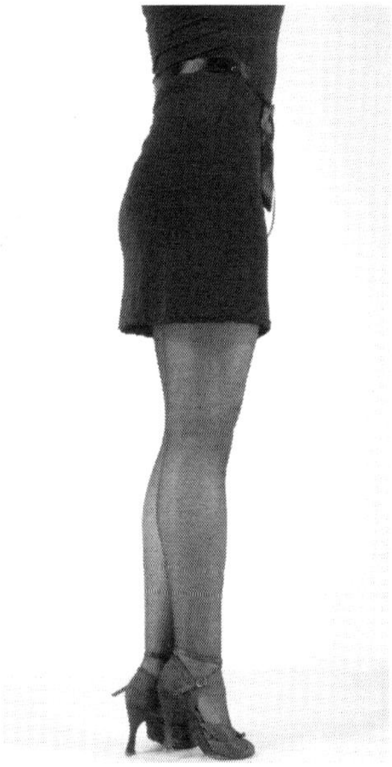

Start in Rumba poise with feet together and slightly turned out, with ankles touching.

Extend arms to the side at shoulder level, slightly forward and flexed, with palms of the hands facing downward.

Move almost full weight onto RF, locking R knee.

Settle to R by allowing hips to move slightly to R and rotate diagonally backwards.

6a

On Count 4

Commence to transfer part weight (approximately 50%) onto LF by lowering L heel.

R knee is still locked and RF flat.

6b

On Count &

Continue to transfer more weight (approximately 70%) from RF to LF.

Release heel of RF from the floor, keeping R knee straight.

Commence to straighten L knee slightly and to move hips diagonally L and forwards.

Keep same height throughout whole exercise.

> This exercise develops the timing and continuity of the weight change for closed feet using the settling action from the previous exercise.

6c

On Count 1

Continue to transfer more weight (approximately 90%) onto LF by fully straightening knee.

Both knees are now straight, but not locked, and hips are level.

Feel how body weight appears to be towards the ball of the LF, with some pressure on inside edge of ball of RF.

6d

On Count &

Transfer almost full weight onto L leg, locking L knee.

Settle to L by allowing hips to move slightly to L and rotate diagonally backwards. Feel how body weight appears to be near the heel of LF.

Allow the knee of the R leg to flex forwards, keeping ankles touching.

The hips have now completed half of a figure of eight, from diagonally backward to R to forward and then diagonally backward to L.

Repeat on RF using Counts 2, &, 3, &. Then with slow Rumba music taking 1 beat for each weight change using Counts 1&, 2&, 3&, 4&.

Or combine into 2 quick weight changes (Counts 2&, 3&) with 1 slow (Counts 4, &, 1,& as described in exercise).

Rumba | Backward foot extension and settling

7 This exercise develops the coordination between the body axis, moving leg and hip action (settling) as used, for example, in the Forward Walks. This and the next two exercises are also useful for Cha cha cha.

Start in Rumba poise with feet together and knees straight but not locked.

Place both hands on pelvis or extend arms to the side at shoulder level, slightly forward and flexed, with palms of the hands facing downward.

7a

On Count 1

Transfer almost full weight onto RF and extend LF back on inside edge of toe with some pressure into the floor.

Achieve position with both knees locked, hips level with the floor and slightly rotated to L.

7b

On Count &

Move the body axis slightly forwards.

Settle to R by allowing hips to move slightly to R and rotate diagonally backwards.

At the same time, bend L leg and close LF to RF without weight change, using the inside edge of the toe then the ball of the foot with some pressure into the floor, with ankles touching.

Return to position of Photo 7a and repeat on RF using the Counts 2 & 3 & 4 &

Repeat on LF.

Then to Rumba or slow Cha cha cha music.

Rumba | Forward foot extension and settling

This exercise develops the coordination between the body axis, leg movement and hip action (settling), as used in the Backward Walk.

Start in Rumba poise with feet together and knees straight but not locked.

Place both hands on pelvis or extend arms to the side at shoulder level, slightly forward and flexed, with palms of the hands facing downward.

8a

On Count 1

Take almost full weight on LF and extend RF forwards on toe, turned slightly out, with some pressure into the floor.

Achieve position with both knees locked, hips level with the floor and facing forward.

8b

On Count &

Move the body axis slightly backwards towards L heel without affecting the body's poise.

Settle to L by allowing hips to move slightly to L and rotate diagonally backwards.

At the same time, close RF to LF without weight change, using centre of toe, then inside edge of ball of foot with some pressure into the floor, with ankles touching.

Return to position in Photo 8a and repeat on LF using Counts 2 & 3 & 4 &

Repeat on RF.

Then to Rumba or slow Cha cha cha music.

9

This exercise develops the coordination between the body axis, moving leg and hip action (settling) as used, for example, in Side Steps and Side Cucarachas. The different motion helps focus attention on ensuring the movement is accurate.

Start in Rumba poise with feet together and knees straight but not locked.

Extend arms to the side at shoulder level, slightly forward and flexed, with palms of the hands facing downward. Alternatively, place hands on pelvis or hip joints.

9a

On Count 1

Transfer almost full weight onto LF and extend RF to side with some pressure on toe turned out.

Achieve position with both knees locked, hips level to the floor slightly rotated to the R.

9b

On Count &

Move the body axis slightly to L.

Settle to L by allowing hips to move slightly to L and rotate diagonally backwards.

At the same time, close RF to LF without weight change, using the inside edge of the toe then the ball of the foot with some pressure into the floor, with ankles touching.

Return to position in Photo 9a and continue by repeating exercise on LF using the Counts 2 & 3 & 4 &.

Repeat on RF. Then to Rumba or slow Cha cha cha music.

(The optional rotation of the elbow shown in Photo 9b is described in Ex.38.)

Cha cha cha Exercises

Cha cha cha has a clear staccato rhythm and cheeky character. Dancers need to find a way to be quick and precise while looking carefree. In many steps, rhythm is expressed through straightening the knees and lowering the heels at the beginning of each beat of music.

This set of exercises develops the basic actions in Cha cha cha. In addition Rumba Exercises 5, 7, 8 and 9 are also useful and later sets of exercises for the Rotations, Arms and Combination further develop coordinated precise movement.

10 The aim of this exercise to develop the slight tilting of the pelvis used in Cha cha cha without changing either the position of the body or height. A slight tilting of the pelvis is used in the different kinds of Chassé and >

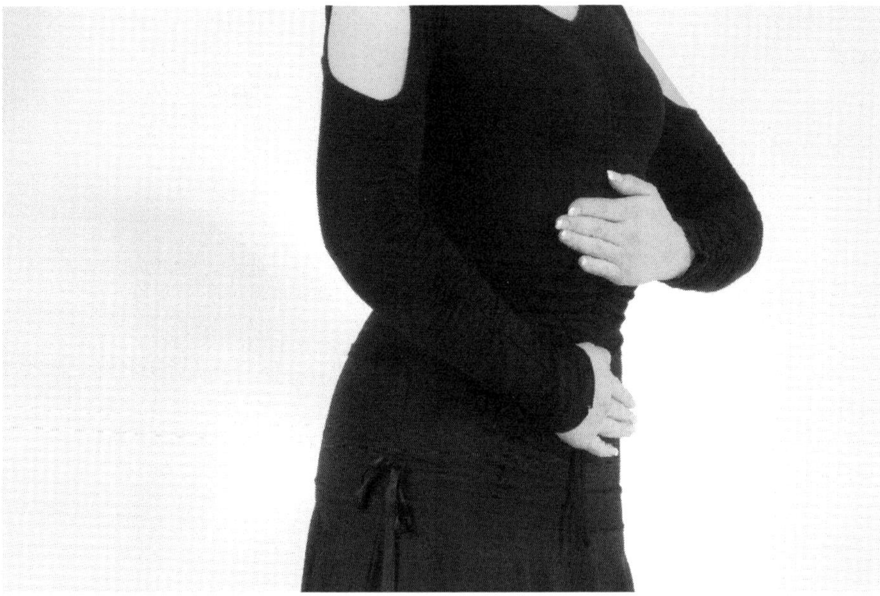

Start in Cha cha cha poise with feet together and slightly turned out, heels touching.

Straighten and lock both knees, keeping weight equally distributed on both feet.

Place R hand on stomach and L hand above it on diaphragm (see above).

> the Locks Forward and Backward in order to be able to continue body movement while closing, half closing or crossing the feet in $^1/_2$ beat of music.

10a

On Count &

Contract abdominal and glute muscles so that the pelvis is tilted forwards.

Allow the knees to flex very slightly, following the tilting of the pelvis.

As a result the hands touch or almost touch each other.

Ensure thighs and knees stay in contact.

10b

On Count 1

Return to starting position.

Keep the same height, the spine straight and upper part of body still throughout the exercise.

Continue by repeating exercise using Counts &1, &2, &3, &4.

Then use Cha cha cha music.

Optionally repeat exercise with feet in Latin Cross position (one crossed behind the other, on inside edge of ball with toe turned out).

Cha cha cha | Hip action

11 The settling action for Cha cha cha is similar to the Rumba, but the transfer of weight is quicker and the pelvis tilts slightly forwards between settling to either side.

Start in Cha cha cha poise with feet together and slightly turned out, heels touching, with both knees straight, but not locked, and weight equally distributed on both feet.

Extend arms to the side at shoulder level, slightly forward and flexed, with palms of the hands facing downward.

Throughout the exercise, ensure that the position of the upper part of the body is not affected, the same height is maintained and the spine kept straight. This is achieved by:

- stretching spine upwards
- tightening the *gluteus muscles* (glutes) and abdominal core muscles
- keeping shoulders facing forward.

11a

On Count &

Transfer almost full weight onto RF, locking R knee and settle to R by allowing the hips to move slightly to the R and rotate diagonally backwards.

Allow knee of L leg to flex, ensuring it remains facing forward, with LF on inside edge of ball with some pressure, ankles touching.

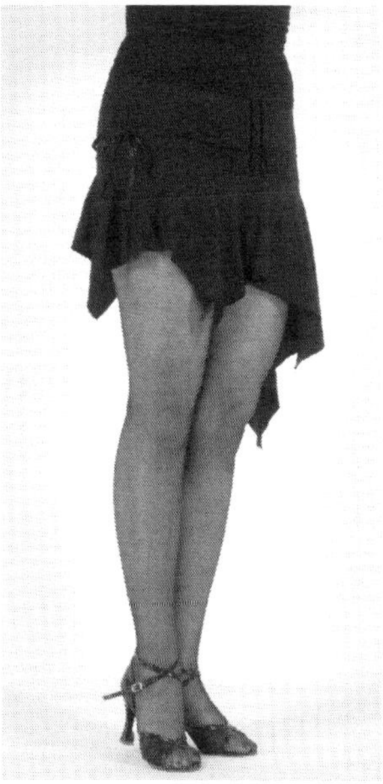

11b

On Count 1

Start to transfer weight to L by lowering LF, unlocking R knee and releasing heel of RF from the floor, with weight distributed over the balls of the feet.

As heel of RF comes off the floor, hips start to rotate.

Engage glutes and abdominal muscles to tilt pelvis slightly forwards achieving a central and level position (as described in previous Exercise 10).

11c

On Count &

Continue to transfer weight onto LF, locking L knee, and settle to L by allowing hips to move slightly to L and rotate diagonally backwards, completing a half circle.

Allow knee of R leg to flex, ensuring it remains facing forward, with RF on inside edge of ball with some pressure into the floor, ankles touching.

Repeat on LF and RF alternatively using Counts & 1 & 2 & 3 & 4.

Then to Cha cha cha music doubling the speed of transfer of weight on 4 & 1.

12

This is an exercise to develop precise Cha cha cha Side Chassés as used in many figures and, in particular, to keep the same height during the whole Chassé. Maintaining the same height is achieved by the pelvis tilting >

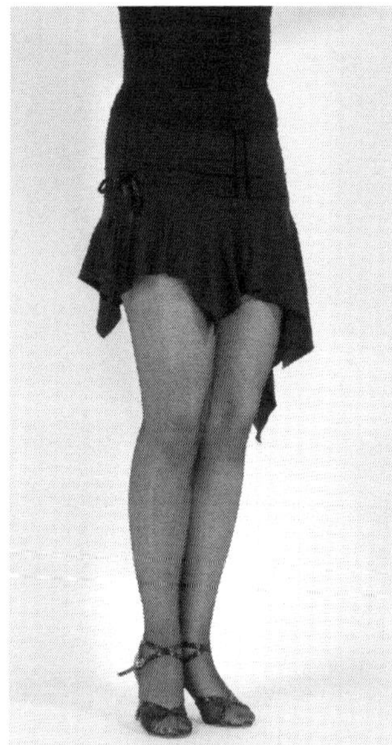

Start in Cha cha cha poise with feet together and slightly turned out, arms extended to side.

On Count &

Transfer almost full weight onto LF, locking L knee, and settle to L by allowing hips to move slightly L and rotate diagonally backwards.

Allow R knee to flex facing forward, RF on inside edge of ball with some pressure, ankles touching.

12a

On Count 4

Take RF to side with a small step (approximately 1/2 shoulder width, because of the 1/2 beat of music) with knee compressed, using inside edge of ball of foot then place flat.

12b

On Count &

Close (or half close) LF to RF with toes slightly turned out, ball of foot then flat, with ankles touching.

Ensure both knees are towards each other, slightly compressed.

Continue to rotate hips to a central position and tilt pelvis slightly forwards.

> slightly forwards to compensate for the compression of both knees on the second step and a slight rotation of the hips when straightening them on the third step.

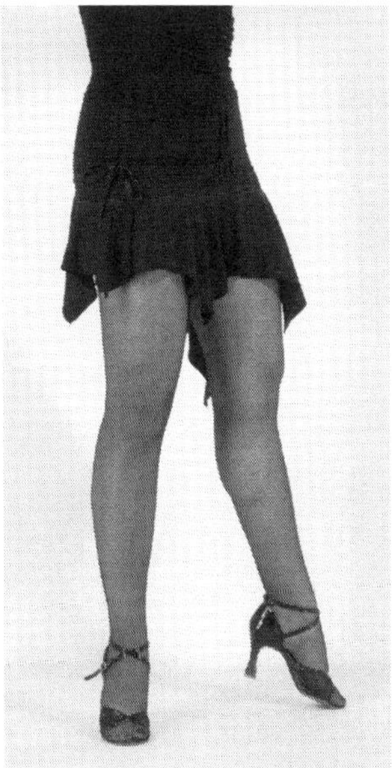

12c

On Count 1

Take RF to side. Step is bigger than previous (approximately shoulder width because of the whole and accented beat of music) with RF on inside edge of ball then flat.

Lock both knees.

Keep hips level to the floor and allow hips to rotate slightly to L.

Release heel of LF and point toe with some pressure allowing it to turn out and remain in same place (avoid any sliding of the LF on the floor, except for the wide Chassé in Cross Basic).

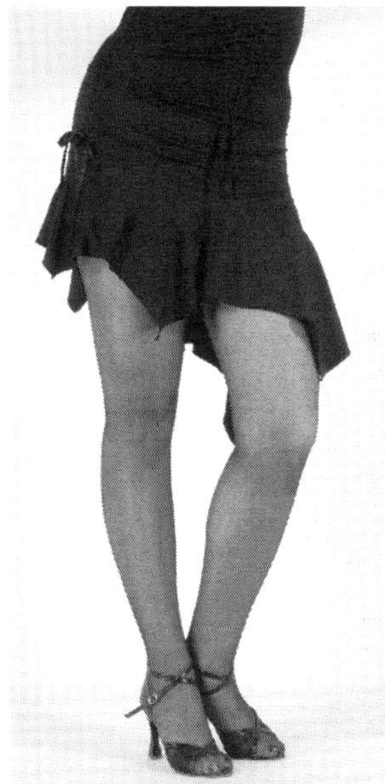

12d

On Count &

Settle to R by allowing hips to move slightly to R and rotate diagonally backwards.

Close LF to RF without weight change, LF on inside edge of ball with some pressure, ankles touching.

On Counts 2, 3

Hold

Repeat exercise on LF & RF alternately, using Counts 4& 1& and holding 2, 3 or Cha cha cha music.

Repeat gradually turning up to 1/4 to R or L during the whole Side Chassé.

Practise both Compact Side Chassé, using steps almost in place, and Wide Side Chassé, using longer steps as used in Cross basic.

13

When watching Latin dancers, I often see them transfer too much weight onto their front foot in Checks and lose control of the movement. This overbalances them, affects connection with their partners and delays >

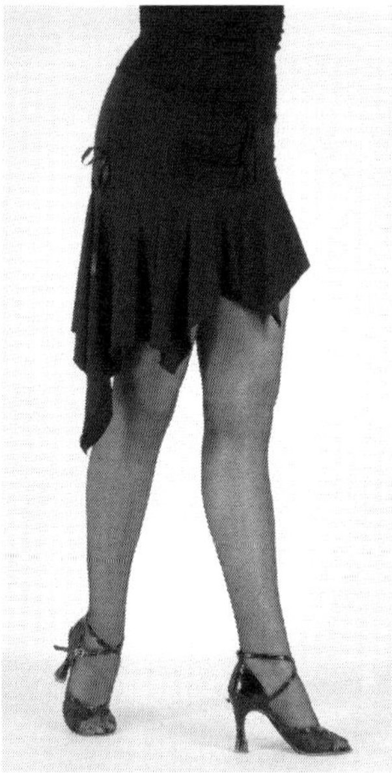

Start in Cha cha cha poise with feet together and slightly turned out, arms extended to side.

On Count &
Transfer almost full weight onto RF, locking R knee, and settle to R by allowing hips to move slightly to R and rotate diagonally backwards.

Allow L knee to flex facing forward, LF on inside edge of ball with some pressure, ankles touching.

13a
On Count 2
Take a step forwards with LF, toe turned out, on ball of foot then flat, with part body weight (approximately 50% of body weight) and RF on inside edge of ball with pressure (50% of body weight).

Lock both knees.

13b
On Count &
Continue to transfer body weight to LF (no more than 70%)

Flex the R knee to tuck to side and behind L knee (ensure it doesn't pass forward of the L knee).

Allow the hips to settle to L by moving slightly to L and rotating diagonally backwards, weight felt to be near heel of LF on the last part of the Count &.

RF on inside edge of ball with pressure into the floor (at least 30% of body weight).

> the next step, taking it slightly out of time and so losing the precision needed in Cha cha cha. This exercise uses the Checked Forward Walk to develop the correct normal weight transfer. The same exercise can be used for Rumba. 13

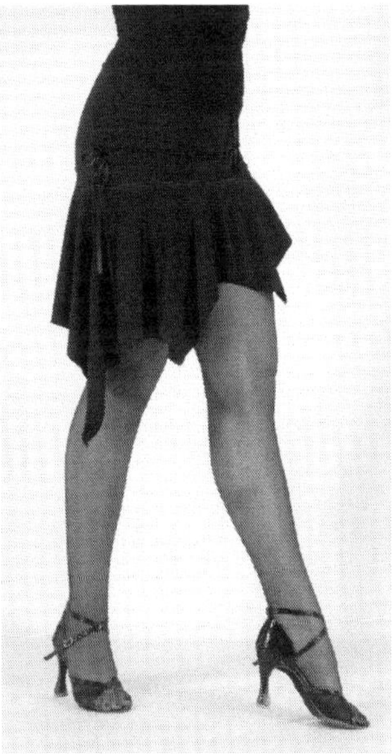

13c

On Count 3

Transfer weight back to RF (approximately 90%) using inside edge of ball then flat, straighten R knee, and release heel of LF retaining some pressure on toe (10%).

Centre and level hips.

Ensure the body remains slightly forward by engaging abdominal core muscles.

13d

On Count &

Complete almost full weight transfer to RF, locking R knee, and settle to R by allowing hips to move slightly to R and rotate diagonally backwards.

At the same time, close LF to RF without weight change, LF on inside edge of ball with some pressure, ankles touching, L knee bending.

Repeat stepping forward with LF.

Then change weight and step forward with RF using the same Count as described.

Also do exercise to Cha cha cha or Rumba music using Counts 2 & 3 & and holding for Counts 4 & 1 &.

Note: Some advanced competitive dancers step forward in a Forward Walk, often changing the timing, in order to create a big body movement before transforming it into a Checked Forward Walk, but this requires high level body control.

14

In the Last Backward Walk in Cha cha cha and Rumba, almost full weight is transferred gradually onto the back foot, with the front knee straight (as used, for example in Close and Open Basic Movements and in Hand >

Start in Cha cha cha poise with feet together and slightly turned out, arms extended to side.

On Count &
Transfer almost full weight onto LF, locking L knee, and settle to L.

14a
On Count 2
Take RF back (no more than a shoulder-width), inside edge of ball then flat, and lock R knee.

Ensure body stays slightly forward with engaged abdominal muscles.

Keep L knee locked and release heel of LF and point toe with some pressure allowing it to turn out slightly and remain in same place (avoid any sliding of the LF on the floor).

14b
On Count &
Settle to R by allowing hips to move slightly to R and rotate diagonally backwards, weight felt to be near heel of RF on the last part of the Count &.

At the time of settling, commence to move L side of body forwards.

L knee is still locked, with some pressure on L toe.

Keep head and shoulders facing forward.

> to Hand). The purpose of the exercise is to improve the timing of the weight transfer and settling of the Last Backward Walk, as a common fault is to settle too early which results in the front knee flexing and delaying the next step Forward in Place.

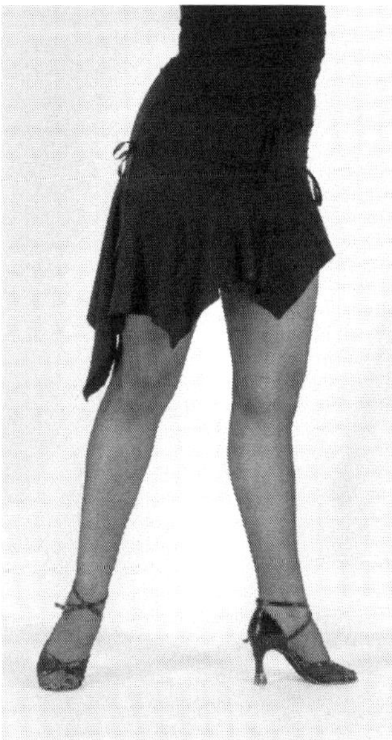

14c

On Count 3

Transfer almost full weight forwards onto LF on ball then flat.

Release heel of RF from the floor, allowing the foot to rotate outwards onto inside edge of ball then toe with some pressure.

Keep both knees locked.

Hips are level with the floor and diagonal to the wall.

14d

On Count &

Settle to L by allowing hips to move slightly to L and rotate diagonally backwards.

At the same time close RF to LF without weight change, RF on inside edge of ball with some pressure, ankles touching.

Repeat using RF using Counts 2 & 3 & and holding Counts 4 & 1 &.

Change weight and repeat using LF back using same Counts.

Then to Cha cha cha or Rumba music.

Samba Exercises

Samba music has a rhythm that is naturally expressed in dance through a bounce and pelvis action. The aim of this set of exercises is to develop a continuous and nicely sprung movement. They help strengthen and coordinate the groups of muscles needed for soft bounce, flexibility around the pelvis and correct slip action.

Samba | **Bounce action**

15 This exercise develops the bounce action in place, before using it in steps and figures. In particular, the exercise seeks to maintain the same vertical body position, avoiding any tilting backwards or forwards. It also >

Start in Samba poise with feet together and parallel, weight equally distributed on both feet towards balls.

Place hands on sides of waist or hip joint.

15a

On Count & (or 1)

Compress both knees, keeping the spine straight and vertical.

Keep feet flat.

15b

On Count 1 (or &)

Rise onto the balls of the feet, keeping the spine straight and vertical.

Both knees are straight but not locked.

> strengthens muscles in the feet, ankles, calves and thighs. There are alternative timings for the Samba bounce action and both are given for the exercise.

15c

On Count & (or 2)

Lower heel, then feet flat, and compress both knees, keeping the spine straight and vertical.

15d

On Count 2 (or &)

Rise onto the balls of the feet, keeping the spine straight and vertical.

Both knees are straight but not locked.

The bounce movement should be continuous throughout the exercise at any speed - there are no stops at any point.

Repeat the exercise counting & 1 & 2 or 1 & 2 & or to Samba music.

For advanced dancers, optionally repeat with weight on one foot, holding the other in contact with the standing leg at calf level with toe pointing down (see photos 4c, d).

16

Pelvis action is added to the bounce action of the previous exercise through use of the abdominal, side of back and glute muscle groups. The movement includes a rotation of the pelvis diagonally back with hip-lift, >

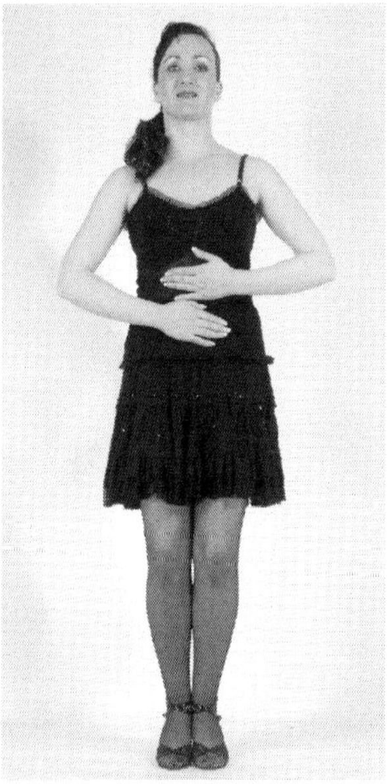

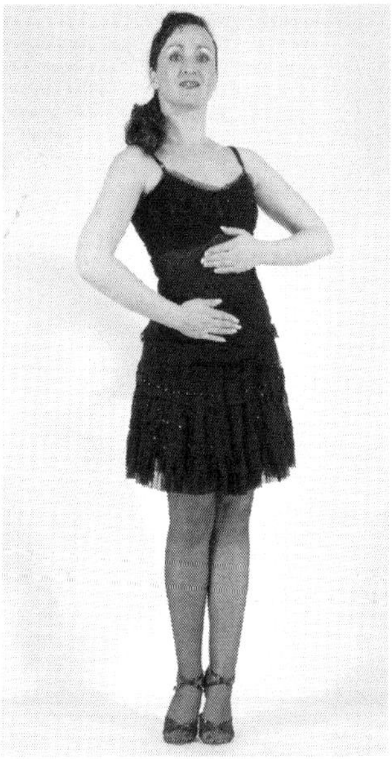

Start in Samba poise with feet together and parallel, weight equally distributed on both feet towards balls.

Place L hand on diaphragm and R hand on stomach.

16a

On Count & (or 1)
Compress both knees, keeping them in contact with each other.

Tilt pelvis forwards and upwards by contracting the abdominal, hamstring and glute muscles.

As a result, the hands should touch, or almost touch, each other.

Ensure that the upper body stays vertical throughout the exercise and, as far as possible, facing the same direction.

16b

On Count 1 (or &)
Rise onto balls of both feet.

Both knees straight (L knee slightly more because of the rotation of the pelvis to L), but not locked.

Rotate pelvis L and diagonally backwards.

Lift the L hip by contracting the muscles along the L side and back.

As a result, the distance between the hands is bigger than in their starting position.

> without affecting the position of the upper body. The action is used, for example, in all types of Samba Walks and optionally in other figures.

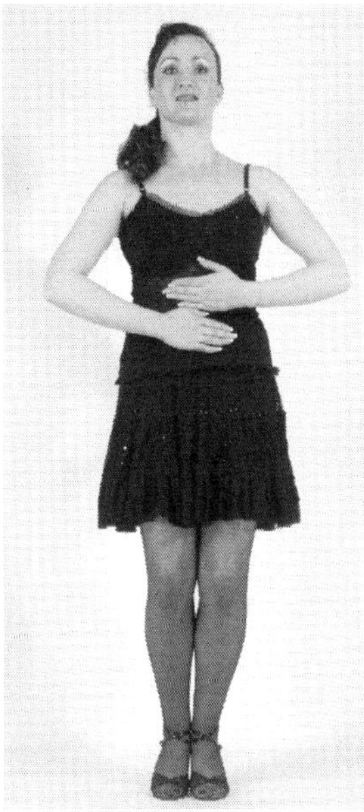

16c

On Count & (or 2)

Compress both knees, keeping them in contact with each other.

Tilt pelvis forwards and upwards by contracting the abdominal, hamstring and glute muscles.

As a result, the hands should touch, or almost touch, each other.

16d

On Count 2 (or &)

Rise onto balls of both feet.

Both knees straight (R knee slightly more because of the rotation of the pelvis to R), but not locked.

Rotate pelvis R and diagonally backwards.

Lift the R hip by contracting the muscles along the R side and back.

As a result, the distance between the hands is bigger than in their starting position.

Note how the pelvis moves in a half circle between the L and R diagonally backward positions.

Repeat the exercise counting & 1 & 2 or 1 & 2 & or to Samba music.

Samba | Weight change to side and in place

17

The purpose of this exercise is to learn change of weight, first from a side step and then in place, in order to match Samba timing accurately (1 & a 2, using 1/4 beat for 'a'). Weight change in place is used in many basic >

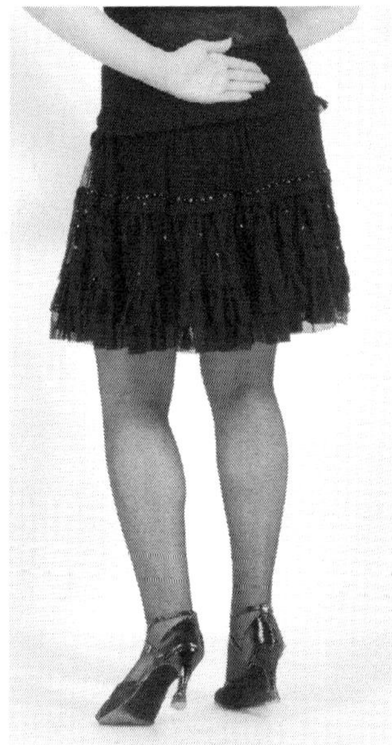

Start in Samba poise with feet together and parallel, knees straight but not locked, and weight on RF.

Place R palm on lower abdomen and L palm on lower part of the back facing out in order to better feel and control the tilting and rotation of pelvis.

17a

On Count &

Compress both knees.

Tilt pelvis forwards and slightly upwards (as described in previous Exercise 16).

17b

On Count a

Commence to rise onto balls of both feet by releasing heels from the floor without straightening knees.

Rotate pelvis slightly to R.

Take a small step to L side with LF, with part weight (approximately 50%), inside edge of ball of foot then ball.

> figures, for example in Natural, Reverse and Progressive Basic Movements. The exercise is also useful as preparation for Volta movements.

17c

On Count 1

Rise onto balls of both feet, straighten both knees without locking and transfer full weight onto LF.

Close RF with part weight to LF (approximately 50%).

Rotate pelvis to L and diagonally backwards and lift L hip upwards, without affecting the position of the upper body.

Continue from Photo 17b counting a 2, and then repeat using Counts & a 1 & a 2.

Repeat to R.

17d

On Count &

Transfer full weight to RF on ball then flat.

Compress both knees.

Tilt pelvis forwards and slightly upwards.

Repeat to L and R using Counts as described and then Samba music.

It is also useful to repeat in place with LF and RF, using Counts then Samba music.

18

In the Samba slip, it's important that the leg that does the slipping action moves in contact with the floor with foot flat, the correct partial weight is transferred onto the back foot, and the body from rib-cage up is >

Start in Samba poise with feet together and parallel, with weight on RF.

Extend arms to the side at shoulder level, slightly forward and flexed, with palms of R hand facing downward and palm of L hand upward, with fingers shaped.

Alternatively place hands on hip joints.

On Count &
Compress knees and tilt pelvis forwards and upwards.

18a
On Count a
Extend LF backwards with straight knee, big step, with part weight on inside edge of toe with toe turned out.

Begin to rotate pelvis diagonally backwards, ensuring that the position of the upper body is not affected.

> unaffected by the pelvis action. The purpose of this exercise is to develop the correct movement with slight bounce and pelvis action in good balance and precise timing.

18b

On Count 2

Continue to transfer more weight onto LF, pushing from RF by straightening R knee without locking.

Lift L hip by contracting the muscles on the L side and back of the body (between armpit and hip).

As a result RF slips back on flat foot with some pressure into the floor.

(The amount of slip would usually be less than half the length of the foot and stop under the core, depending on size of backward step and degree of weight transfer and pelvis action.)

Immediately after the slip, pelvis begins to move forwards.

18c

On Count &

Compress R knee, keeping L knee straight with toe of LF turning out.

Allow pelvis to return to position parallel to the floor and diagonal to the wall, following which the L toe may turn out slightly further.

To repeat on same leg:
Hold on Counts 1 & then flex L knee slightly, tilting pelvis forwards, and continue as described on Counts a 2 &.

Repeat on other leg, by returning to starting position, change weight and extend RF backwards and continue as described above.

Use Counts then Samba music.

19

The action for the side slip follows the same principles as for the back slip, but in another direction so different muscle groups (particularly the adductors in the inner thigh) are used to create the slip.

Start in Samba poise with feet together and parallel, with weight on LF.

Place hands on hip joints. Alternatively extend arms to the side at shoulder level, slightly forward and flexed, with palms facing downward.

On Count &
Compress knees and tilt pelvis forwards and slightly upwards.

19a

On Count a
Extend RF to side with straight knee, big step, with part weight on inside edge of toe with toe turned out.

Begin to rotate pelvis diagonally rightwards and backwards, ensuring that the position of the upper body is not affected.

19b

On Count 2

Continue to transfer more weight onto RF, pushing from LF by straightening L knee without locking.

Lift R hip by contracting the muscles on the R side and back of the body (between armpit and hip).

As a result LF slips rightwards on flat foot with some pressure into the floor.

(The amount of slip would usually be less than half the length of the foot and stop under the core, depending on size of sideway step, degree of weight transfer and pelvis movement.)

Immediately after the slip, pelvis commences to move leftwards.

19d

On Count &

Compress L knee, keeping R knee straight with toe of RF turned out.

Allow pelvis to return to position parallel to the floor and diagonal to the wall,following which the R toe may turn out slightly further.

To repeat on same leg:
Hold on Counts 1 & then flex R knee slightly, tilting pelvis forwards, and continue as described on Counts a 2 &.

Repeat on other leg, by returning to starting position, change weight and extend LF to side and continue as described above.

Use Counts then Samba music.

Jive Exercises

Jive expresses joy of life, lightness and fun. A swing action with soft springy foot, ankle and knee movement help to attain a higher speed and project the character of the dance.

Almost all Jive figures contain Chassés and Rock Actions, and the following exercises focus on these while developing a precise and good technique.

Jive | Side swing action

20 The Jive swing action is a pendulum movement of the body with weight change, moving as a single block from the hip joints to the crown of the head, with the feeling of the pelvis acting as the weight of the pendulum.

Start in Jive poise, with feet apart, weight equally distributed towards the balls, and knees slightly bent.

Place hands on pelvis at the level of the hip joint to better feel the pendulum movement of the hips.

Focus throughout on using the inside edges of the feet and ensure that the weight does not move beyond the centre of the standing foot (beware of rolling out).

20a
On Count 1
Transfer body weight to RF and swing hips to R, allowing body sway to L.

Release L heel from the floor, pressure on inside edge of ball of LF, with L knee and ankle slightly inwards.

20b
On Count &
Start to swing hips and body to L passing through neutral position where weight is equally distributed with both feet flat and spine perpendicular to the floor.

On Count 2
Continue to swing and transfer body weight to LF, allowing body sway to R.

Release R heel from the floor, pressure on inside edge of ball of RF, with R knee and ankle slightly inwards.

Repeat, swinging to alternate sides using Counts 1 & 2 & 3 & 4.
Check, if necessary, by looking in a mirror, that the sides of the body do not bend and hips do not settle as in Rumba and Cha cha cha.

A good swing action enables continuity of motion and facilitates quick changes of direction of movement, for example between Chassés. Another advantage of an effective swing is that the body's momentum gives greater foot speed while expending less energy.

Start with the previous Exercise 20.

21a

On Count 1

Continue to swing the hips to R and allow body to sway to L.

Add slight bounce action through straightening (but not locking) R knee, foot flat.*

This allows the hips to swing further and LF to close to R calf with L knee bent facing forward.

Point the L toe downward approximately at the level of the ankle (height will depend on amount of swing, bounce and hip action).

21b

On Count &

Replace LF on floor to side, inside edge of ball then flat.

Swing hips and body to L passing through neutral position where weight is equally distributed with both feet flat and spine perpendicular to the floor.

On Count 2

Continue to swing the hips to L and allow body to sway to R with foot collection of RF to calf of L leg with R knee bent, facing forward.

Point the R toe downward at the level of the ankle.

Repeat, swinging to alternate sides using Counts 1 & 2 & 3 & 4.
**For more advanced dancers, add slight foot rise on the standing leg, through the ankle releasing the heel from the floor, at the end of Counts 1 and 2.*

22 Jive | Diagonal swing action

This exercise develops the diagonal swing action moving in a forward and backward direction.

Start in Jive poise, with feet apart with LF forward, toe pointing forward, and RF back with toe slightly turned out, weight equally distributed, and knees slightly flexed.

Place hands on pelvis at the level of the hip joint.

22a

On Count 1

Transfer body weight forwards onto LF and swing hips diagonally forwards to L, allowing body to sway slightly diagonally R.

Release heel of RF with some pressure on inside edge of toe.

22b

On Count &

Commence to transfer weight backwards to RF.

Start to swing hips diagonally backwards to R passing through neutral position where weight is equally distributed with both feet flat, spine perpendicular to the floor.

On Count 2

Continue to transfer weight backwards onto RF and to swing hips R and diagonally backwards, allowing body to sway slightly to L and diagonally forwards.

Release heel of LF with some pressure on inside edge of toe.

Repeat, swinging forwards and backwards, with Counts 1 & 2 & 3 & 4. The body should move as a single block (or plank) from the hip joints to the crown of the head. Check, if necessary, by looking in a mirror.

Jive | Diagonal swing with foot collection

23

The purpose is to combine the swing action of Exercise 22 with a slight bounce action and immediate transfer of weight from forward and backward onto the standing leg, which together then causes foot collection lifting off the floor.

Start with the previous Exercise 22

23a

On Count 1

Continue to swing the hips and body as a unit, from R diagonally backward to L diagonally forward.

Transfer full weight onto the standing L leg and add slight bounce action through straightening L knee, foot flat.*

This allows the hips to swing further, resulting in RF closing to L ankle with R knee bent facing forward (foot collection). Point the R toe downward.

23b

On Count &

Take a step RF backwards, inside edge of ball then flat.

Swing hips and body diagonally back passing through neutral position.

On Count 2

Continue to swing hips R and diagonally backwards and transfer full weight onto the standing R leg and add slight bounce to result in foot collection. Point the L toe downward.

Repeat with Counts 1 & 2 & 3 & 4.

Repeat using RF forward and LF backward.

**For advanced dancers, add slight foot rise on the standing foot at the end of Counts 1 and 2.*

24

Most basic Jive figures contain Chassés. The intention of this exercise is to learn to combine the swing and slight bounce action during a Chassé step in order to increase foot speed and lightness of movement. >

Start in Jive poise with feet apart, weight equally distributed towards the balls, and knees slightly bent. Place hands on pelvis at the level of the hip joint.

Swing hips to L and allow slight body sway to R, and RF to close to calf of L leg with toe pointing downward (see Photo 21b).

24a

On Count 1

Bend L knee and commence pelvis swinging to R.

Allow the movement of the swing to R to enable a small side step on RF on inside edge of ball, keeping it under the body (approximately half a shoulder width). Slightly bend R knee, with part weight.

24b

On Count a

Half close (nearly together) LF on ball of foot to RF.

Straighten both knees slightly, but do not lock.

Continue to swing pelvis to R, but at this stage it is still positioned slightly to L.

> In particular helps develop the correct 3/4, 1/4, 1 beat value (counting 1 a 2 or Q a Q) required. In the Side Chassés to R and L, the sway will be slight because it is optionally combined with use of side extension of the upper body in the direction of movement opposite to the hips.

24c

On Count 2

Take a normal step to R (about a shoulder width), with RF on ball then flat.

Bend both knees some more.

Continue to swing pelvis to R, passing through a position where it is central and almost level with the floor.

24d

At the end of Count 2

Straighten R knee, but do not lock.

Complete swing of pelvis to R, allowing body slight sway to L and LF to close to calf of R leg, with toe pointing downward.

Keep RF flat or flat then ball or toe.*

Repeat with Chassé to L, counting 3a4.

**More advanced dancers, repeat with foot rise releasing heel of standing leg from the floor at the end of Counts 2 and 4 (as shown in Photo 24d).*

Note: *There are different ways of counting Jive figures including:*
Q Q QaQ QaQ
1 2 3a4 3a4
1 2 3a4 5a6
For the purpose of this exercise 1a2 3a4 are used, but choose whatever is most appropriate.

25

In the Jive Chassés to L and R, the steps are in the same direction as the swing. In the Forward Chassé the steps are forwards, but the swing is diagonal. The purpose of this exercise is to combine swing, bounce >

Start in Jive poise with feet apart RF forward, LF back, weight equally distributed towards the balls, and knees slightly bent.

Swing hips L and diagonally back and allow body to sway slightly to R and diagonally forwards, upper body to commence forward movement, and RF to close to calf of L leg with toe pointing downward.

25a

On Count 1

Bend L knee and commence pelvis swinging to R and diagonally forwards.

Allow the movement of the swing to enable a small step forwards on inside edge of ball, keeping it under the body. Slightly bend R knee, with part weight.

25a

On Count a

Half close LF to RF (nearly together, toe of LF to instep of RF) on inside edge of ball.

Straighten both knees slightly, but do not lock.

Continue to swing pelvis to R and diagonally forwards, but at this stage it is still positioned slightly to L and diagonally back.

> action and foot collection in the development of the correct timing for Forward Chasses RLR and LRL.

25c

On Count 2

Take a normal step forwards (about a shoulder width), with RF ball then flat.

Bend both knees some more.

Continue to swing pelvis to R and diagonally forwards, passing through a position where it is diagonal with wall and level with the floor.

25d

At the end of Count 2

Straighten R knee, but do not lock.

Complete swing of pelvis to R and diagonally forward, allowing slight body sway to L and diagonally backward and LF to close to calf of R leg, with toe pointing downward.

Keep RF flat or flat then ball or toe.*

Repeat the same on LF or straight into a Backward Chassé (next Exercise 26) counting 3a4.

**More advanced dancers, repeat with foot rise at the end of Counts 2 and 4 (as shown in Photo 25d) for a lighter and more springy action.*

Note: *There are different ways of counting Jive figures including:*
Q Q QaQ QaQ
1 2 3a4 3a4
1 2 3a4 5a6
For the purpose of this exercise 1a2 3a4 are used, but choose whatever is most appropriate.

26

The purpose of the exercise is to keep the body forward in the correct poise when moving backwards and to train the muscle group activities which are different compared to going forwards. In the Backward Chassé,

Start in Jive poise with feet apart RF forward, LF back, weight equally distributed towards the balls, and knees slightly bent.

Swing hips R and diagonally forwards and allow slight body sway to L and diagonally back and LF to close to calf of R leg with toe pointing downward (see Photo 25d).

26a

On Count 1

Bend R knee and commence pelvis swinging to L and diagonally backwards.

Allow the movement of the swing to enable a small step back on inside edge of ball, keeping it under the body (approximately half a shoulder width).

26b

On Count a

Half close RF to LF (nearly together, heel of RF to instep of LF) on inside edge of ball.

Straighten both knees slightly, but do not lock.

Continue to swing pelvis to L and diagonally back, but at this stage it is still positioned slightly to R and diagonally forward.

the leg is moved in advance of the body, whereas for the Forward Chassé, the body moves first and then the leg.

26c

On Count 2

Take a normal step back (about a shoulder width), with LF ball then flat.

Bend both knees.

Continue to swing pelvis to L and diagonally backwards, passing through a position where it is diagonal with wall and level with the floor.

26d

At the end of Count 2

Straighten L knee, but do not lock.

Complete swing of pelvis to L and diagonally backward, allowing slight body sway to R and diagonally forward and RF to close to calf of L leg, with toe pointing downward.

Keep LF flat or flat then ball or toe.*

Repeat the same on RF or continue immediately with a Forward Chassé RLR counting 3a4.

Combine forwards and backwards in different combinations, for example: Forward LRL RLR Backward LRL RLR, Forward LRL Backward RLR, Forward RLR Backward LRL etc.

**More advanced dancers, repeat with foot rise at the end of Counts 2 and 4 (as shown in Photo 26d) for a lighter and more springy action.*

27

Compared to other Latin dances, Jive has different body weight transfer because of the speed and many changes of direction. The Rock Action has only partial weight transfer onto the back foot, keeping the upper >

Start in Jive poise with weight on RF, with straight leg, pelvis to R, LF closed to calf of R leg with toe pointing downward (see Photo 25d).

Extend arms to the side at chest level, flexed with palms of the hands facing downward, or place hands on pelvis at the level of the hip joint.

27a

On Count 1

Bend R knee.

Take LF a normal step back on inside edge of ball.

Hips commence to rotate to L.

L knee commences to straighten.

27b

On Count &

Straighten L knee, but do not lock, as the heel is lowered.

Bend R knee further, releasing heel from the floor.

Allow hips to continue to rotate to L, without arching the back by engaging the glute muscles.

Keep body axis (upper body) almost over the front foot.

> part of the body slightly forward. The exercise develops the coordination of this with hip rotation, slight bounce, swing action and correct footwork.

27c

On Count 2

Transfer weight onto RF, by lowering heel of RF, and compressing R knee slightly more.

Release LF heel from the floor.

Hips commence to rotate to R.

27d

At the end of Count 2

Straighten R knee and allow the hips to rotate R and slightly diagonally backwards.

As a result of the hip rotation, LF closes to calf of R leg, with toe pointing downward.

Keep RF flat or flat then ball or toe.*

Repeat the Rock Action on LF and then on RF.

Repeat without body rotation (as done in Open Hold) or with body rotation of 1/8 (as in Close Hold).

**More advanced dancers, repeat with foot rise at the end of Count 2 (as shown in Photo 27d).*

Optionally, combine as appropriate with Jive Chassés to L and R to create the Basic in Fallaway or combine with 2 Forward and 2 Backward Chassés in preparation for other figures.

Paso Doble Exercises

The character of the Paso Doble is strong and dynamic in expressing a bullfighter's body lines and movements. It has a very different poise to the other Latin dances and dancers need to develop the muscle groups to set that up and maintain it throughout the dance.

The movement itself is also different to the other Latin dances in lacking hip action, but there is pelvis tilt, body sway and side extension.

In the Paso Doble, the feet play an important role in creating percussive effects on the floor. A distinctive movement is the Appel, being a strong lowering action, replacing of the foot with immediate change of weight that, as a result, may produce a loud audible sound. This role of the feet requires specific strengthening of the muscles in the ankles, calves, thighs and pelvis, which this set of exercises is designed to develop.

28

When dancing Paso Doble the basic poise needs to be maintained throughout in order to express the character of the dance. This exercise >

Start in general poise with feet together and parallel, weight equally distributed over the centre of feet. Straighten both knees, but do not lock.

28a

On Count 1

Place hands on hip joints with palms facing downward. Alternatively place palms on pelvis.

28b

On Count 2

Commence to transfer weight towards the balls of feet.

Tilt the pelvis forwards, allowing knees to flex slightly, with the head retaining the same height.

Start to move the elbows back, with the palms rotating naturally to face the body.

> is to develop the shape of the Paso Doble body line in order to move consistently into the correct strong and balanced poise.

28c

On Count 3

Continue to tilt the pelvis forwards.

Release the heels from the floor.

Weight is fully transferred over the balls of the feet.

Both arms are to side and slightly retracted. Continue to move elbows upwards, keeping them back, forearms down, with shoulders still.

28d

On Count 4

Complete the exercise with weight felt to be well over the balls of the feet. Ensure the body is in a curved line from the balls of the feet to the crown of the head without arching the back.

Move arms upwards and turn elbows to bring hands to front, keeping upper arms slightly retracted at shoulder level.

This is the basic Paso Doble poise.*

On Counts 5,6,7,8
Hold in this poise in order to allow muscle groups to become stronger and familiar with their positions.

Return to starting position, relax and repeat exercise.

**For advanced dancers, at the end of the 8-count exercise, add:*

1–4 Flex knee gradually, tilt pelvis further forwards and shape body further backwards (without arching the back)

5–8 Return gradually to the basic Paso Doble poise. Then return to starting position, relax, and repeat whole exercise.

29

The characteristic body lines of the bullfighter have a strong body curve with sway, side extension and rotation. The exercise helps to develop the appropriate Paso Doble shaping that is used in many figures by both >

Start in Paso Doble poise (see Exercise 28). For less advanced dancers, keep feet flat on the floor.

29a

Face palms outward with elbows backward and shoulders down, showing a strong back and neck line.

Either hold a cape or scarf – or imagine doing so – and pull it tight by pushing outwards, engaging the back muscles and all the arm muscles to the hands.

29b

On Counts 1-4

Move pelvis gradually to R and at the same time rotate upper body to R and diagonally backwards, keeping pelvis tilted forward. This creates body sway to L from the ankle to the crown of the head.

Ensure L side of the body remains extended.

Rotate arms with the upper body.

Keep toes facing the starting direction.

> leaders and followers. Optionally find a scarf or heavy cape to use for this exercise.

29c

On Counts 5–8

Gradually return body and pelvis to starting position without stopping movement.

29d

On Counts 1-4

Repeat the same movement with body rotation to L and sway to R.

On Counts 5–8

Return gradually to starting position.

Repeat exercise counting slower or quicker (using 4 or 2 counts for each movement), rotating less or more according to time.

Then use Paso Doble music.

Optionally repeat keeping arms and shoulders facing forward or rotate upper body in opposite direction to the pelvis.

Optionally repeat with feet apart (shoulder width or more) with weight equally distributed and feet flat.

30

This exercise develops the percussive effect created through the feet when when weight is transferred in place with a foot lift that is then replaced onto the floor with pressure on ball of foot. There are different >

Start in Paso Doble poise, weight equally distributed on balls of feet.

Place both hands on hips.

30a

On Count a (or &)

Transfer weight onto LF.

Move the lower part of R leg backward, keeping both knees and thighs still and in contact.

The photo shows a big backward movement of the lower leg used when the doing the exercise slowly. This would be smaller (about halfway) when done quickly.*

30b

On Count 1

Replace RF on ball with strong pressure into the floor, creating an audible sound.

Transfer part of weight to help maintain balance and the same body axis.

> styles: using only the ankles with a small movement and softer sound, or lifting the lower leg backwards, producing a stronger pressure and louder sound, with easier isolation of foot movement from the upper body.

30c

On Count a (or &)

Transfer weight onto RF on ball.*

Move the lower part of L leg backward, keeping both knees and thighs still and in contact.

30d

On Count 2

Replace LF on ball and strong pressure into the floor, creating an audible sound.

Transfer part of weight.

Aim to retain the same body axis and height throughout the exercise with no movement of the upper body.

Repeat using Counts a 3, a 4 (or & 3, & 4) or 1–8.

Then use Paso Doble music.

Optionally repeat exercise without creating audible sound.

**Beginners may do exercise with flat feet or ball then flat.*

**More advanced dancers optionally use toes of feet throughout, requiring strong ankle and instep muscles with very good balance.*

31

The purpose of this exercise is to develop a stationary Appel as preparation for steps that follow it with a change of body position, for example from Close to Promenade Position or Open Position, or a strong progressive step.

Start in Paso Doble poise, weight equally distributed on balls of feet.

31a

On Count &

Transfer weight onto LF.

Rotate pelvis slightly to R keeping it parallel to floor. The rotation will drive both the stronger replacing of the foot and the subsequent lowering.

On Count a

Move the lower part of R leg backward, keeping both knees and thighs still and in contact.

31b

On Count 1

Drive the pelvis forwards to a level position tilted forward, replacing RF,
- either using ball then flat or flat,
- with or without sound (you can practice both, one soft, another strong).

Immediately lower strongly, both knees compressed, and change weight onto RF.

Hold on Count 2 and rise on Counts 3–4 transfering weight to be equally distributed.

Continue repeating the exercise alternating RF and LF using Counts & a 1, 2, 3–4.
Combine with previous Exercise 30 Sur Place using Counts:1–4 Sur Place
5 Appel
6 Hold
7–8 Rise
Repeat alternating RF and LF.
Then do exercise to Paso Doble music.

Arm Exercises

One of the most noticeable aspects of a dancer is the general shape they create with their body. The arms play a key role in completing good body lines and in presenting its overall shape.

Arms are also an important component in expressing the character of dance. This set of exercises, designed for both leaders and followers, helps to develop the correct feeling for the positions and shaping of the arms and to train muscles before combining them with leg, hip and body movement.

32

This exercise develops a natural and fluid movement of the arm by focusing on the elbow and imagining resistance as if moving the arm through water in swimming.

Start in general poise with feet together with R heel to instep of L foot or alternatively with feet apart.

32a

Extend arms to the side at shoulder level, slightly forward and flexed, with palms of the hands facing downward.

Relax fingers, shaping them:
- with the middle two fingers together and slightly lower than the others (as in photos);
- or shaping with the index finger slightly raised and the other three fingers together,
- or, mostly for leaders, keeping them lightly in contact with each other.

32b

On Counts 2–3

Push elbows downwards gradually, without touching the side of the body.

Allow the wrist to flex and hands to lift slightly.

32c

On Count 4

Commence pulling elbows upwards to approximately 45 degrees, with arm flexed and curved.

Allow the wrist to flex so that the palms face body to continue the same curved arm line.

32d

On Count 1

Continue to pull both elbows to the side and slightly forwards to shoulder level, palms facing downward.

Throughout keep the spine straight, shoulders back, upper arms stretched and elbows as far from the body as possible without locking.

Repeat exercise using both arms then one arm at a time, holding the other still and out to the side in starting position, using Counts 2–3, 4, 1 or 4–1, 2, 3.

Repeat using Rumba or Cha cha cha music.

33

The exercise develops a natural flowing forward movement of the arms, by focusing on the elbow and keeping shoulders still. This will also develop the shoulder, chest and back muscles.

Start in general poise, with feet together with R heel to instep of L foot or alternatively with feet apart.

Extend arms to the side at shoulder level, slightly forward and flexed, with palms of the hands facing downward (see Photo 32a).

Relax the fingers, shaping them with the middle two fingers together and slightly lower than the others (as in photos) or optionally as described in Exercise 32.

33a

On Count &

Rotate both elbows inwards, allowing the palms to turn to face upward.

33b

On Counts 2 –3

Move both elbows forwards gradually towards each other.

Either allow forearms to cross slightly in front of chest (as in photo) or alternatively bring close but do not cross.

33c

On Count &

Rotate both elbows outwards allowing forearms to rotate with arms slightly flexed so that palms face inward toward the body.

33d

On Counts 4–1

Move both elbows backwards gradually to the side and slightly forwards to shoulder level.

At the end of the movement, arms should curve slightly forward and palms will naturally face diagonally downward.

Throughout keep the spine straight, shoulders back, upper arms stretched and elbows as far from the body as possible without locking.

Repeat exercise using both arms then one arm at a time, holding the other still and out to the side in starting position, using Counts &, 2–3, &, 4–1 or &, 4–1, &, 2–3.

Repeat using Rumba or Cha cha cha music.

34

The purpose of this exercise is to combine the two previous ones into a single continuous movement that is frequently used in Rumba and Cha cha cha and also sometimes in Samba, Paso Doble and Jive.

Start as in previous Exercise 33.

34a

On Count &

Rotate both elbows inwards, allowing the palms to turn to face upward.

On Count 2

Move both elbows forwards towards each other until forearms face straight forward.

34b

On Count 3

Rotate elbows outwards, allowing forearms to lower in front to waist level, without touching the body.

Either cross the wrists or alternatively end with fingers pointing towards each other and almost touching.

34c

On Count 1

Commence pulling elbows upwards to approximately 45 degrees, with arm flexed and curved.

Allow the wrist to flex so that the palms face body to continue the same curved arm line.

34d

On Count 1

Continue to pull the elbows to the side and slightly forwards to the starting position.

Throughout keep the spine straight, shoulders back, upper arms stretched and elbows as far from the body as possible without locking.

Repeat exercise with both arms then one arm at the time, the other held in starting position.

Count &2, 3, 4, 1 or use Rumba or Cha cha cha music.

Optionally, use the same sequence with Counts &4, 1, 2, 3 as preparation for Side Cucarachas with Arms. (Exercise 39).

Arms | Upward and Forward Arm Movement

35 The purpose of the exercise is to prepare the arms for movements above the head that are options for followers in figures such as the Open Hip Twist and, for both partners, Checks From Open PP and CPP (New Yorks).

Start as in Exercise 33.

35a

On Count 2

Start to raise both arms leading with the upper arms, allowing wrists to flex slightly so that the palms remain facing downward.

35b

On Count 3

Continue to raise both arms until above head, without touching the head, with arms slightly flexed and palms facing downward and outward.

Keep shoulders down.

35c

On Count &

Rotate elbows and palms inwards.

On Count 4

Lower elbows forwards and down to chest level, with palms towards the face.

Either allow forearms to cross slightly in front of chest (as in photo) or alternatively do not cross.

35d

On Count &

Rotate both elbows outwards, allowing forearms to rotate with arms slightly flexed so that palms face inward.

On Count 1

Move both elbows backwards gradually to the side and slightly forwards at shoulder level.

At the end of the movement, arms should curve slightly forward and palms will naturally face downward.

Repeat exercise with both arms and then one arm at a time, the other held in its starting position using Counts 2, 3, &4, &1 or 4, 1, &2, &3.

It is useful to do exercise in reverse (photos in the order 35d, 35c, 35a), as used in Checks From Open PP and CPP (New Yorks).

Repeat using Rumba, Cha cha cha or any other Latin music.

Arms | Wrist circles

36 Wrist circles are sometimes used by themselves in Paso Doble, developed from the Flamenco influence. As a general exercise, the purpose is improve the flexibility of the wrist and fingers so enabling them to become more expressive.

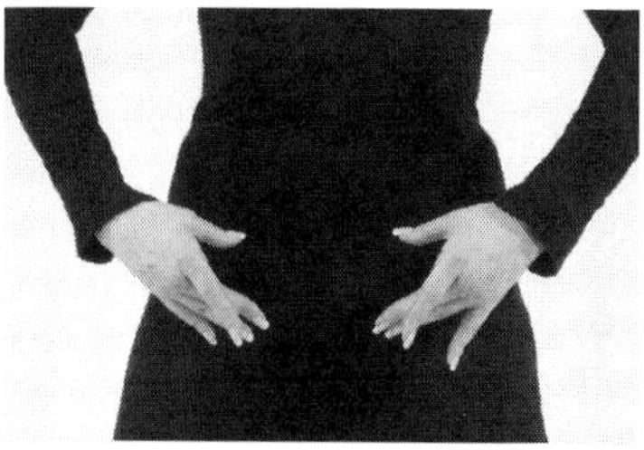

36a

Start in general poise with feet together with R heel to instep of L foot or alternatively with feet apart.

Curve arms in front of the body, hands held in front of abdomen in the same curved

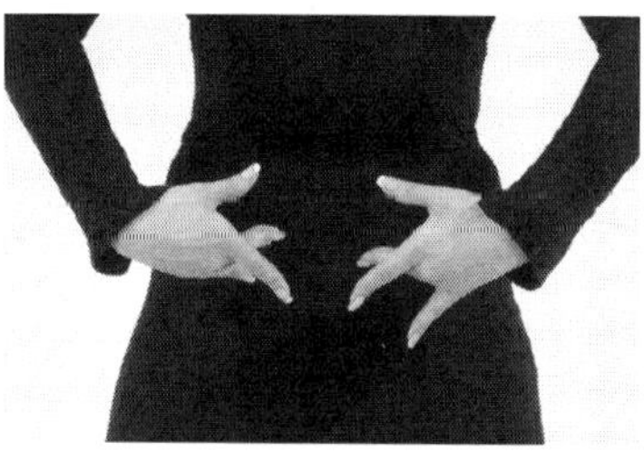

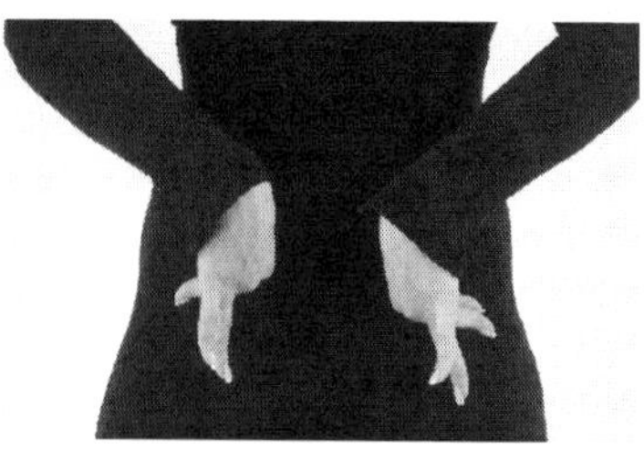

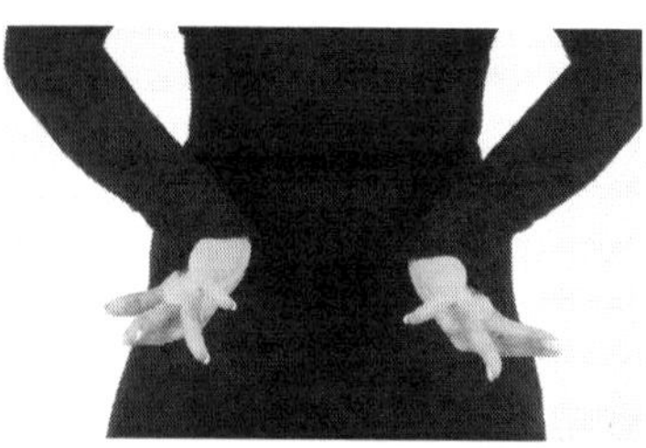

36 b, c, d, e

Rotate palms inwards, downwards and outwards (as in photos), fully flexing the wrist joint.

Keep forearms extended and elbows completely still.

There are options for finger shaping:
- the middle two fingers together and slightly lower than the others (as in Photo 36a)
- start with above shaping, then allow fingers to spread into a fan shape (Photo 36e) as palms face outwards and then return to starting position
- keeping them in contact with each other throughout (mostly for leaders).

Repeat counting 1–4 or 1–8 or using Rumba music for slow and soft movements or Paso Doble music for quick and strong movements.

Repeat exercise reversing movement and rotating inwards, upwards and outwards.

Repeat with hands in different positions and levels:
- *at pelvis level to side (Photo 34c)*
- *at chest level in front (Photo 34a)*
- *at chest level to side (Photo 33d)*
- *above the head (Photo 35b).*

Combination Exercises

This set of exercises help Latin dancers connect the different movements of the parts of the body, in particular the legs, torso and arms. By integrating the actions of each of the muscle groups around the joints from ankle through knee, hips, shoulder, elbow to wrist, movement is completed and looks more natural.

Combination | **Hips and Arms**

37 The purpose of this exercise is to develop the correct feeling of how the different muscle groups connect so that the movement of the arms is felt as the result of weight transfer, settling and body action. The same arm >

Start in Rumba poise with feet together, weight equally distributed, and arms extended to side.

37a

On Count &

Transfer almost full weight to RF, locking R knee, and settle to R by allowing the hips to move slightly to R and rotate diagonally backwards.

Flex L knee, LF on inside edge of ball with some pressure, ankles touching.

Aim to keep the chest facing forward.

Feel how the side stretches as a result of the settling and hip rotation, the shoulder pulls down and so the R elbow naturally wants to rotate inwards and palm to turn to face upward and allow it to do so.

37b

On Count 4

Commence to transfer weight onto LF by lowering the heel.

On Count 1

Pass through the neutral position with knees straight and RF heel slightly released, hips level and both arms in starting position with palms facing downward.

> action can be used in dancing: solo Open Basic Movements Forward and Backward Walks in Rumba and Cha cha cha; Samba Cruzados Walks and Locks; and also in other dances.

37c

On Count &

Transfer almost full weight to LF, locking L knee, and settle to L by allowing the hips to move slightly to L and rotate diagonally backwards.

Flex R knee, RF on inside edge of ball with some pressure, ankles touching.

Aim to keep the chest facing forward.

Feel how the side stretches as a result of the settling and hip rotation, the shoulder pulls down and so the L elbow naturally wants to rotate inwards and palm to turn to face upward and allow it to do so.

37d

On Counts 2

Commence to transfer weight onto RF by lowering the heel.

On Count 3

Pass through the neutral position with knees straight and LF heel slightly released, hips level and both arms in starting position, with palms facing downward.

Ensure the coordination between the body and the arm movement is felt at the moment of settling on Count &.

Repeat using Counts as described or using Counts &, 2–3, &, 4–1, or Rumba or Cha cha cha timing (2, 3, 4&1). Then to Rumba, Cha cha cha or any Latin music.

Combination | Rumba Open Basic with Arms

38 The purpose of this exercise is to connect and coordinate arm movements with steps through weight transfer, settling and hip action. It uses Rumba Open Basic Movement using one or both arms in Forward and >

Start in Rumba poise with almost full weight on RF and extend LF back on inside edge of toe turned out with some pressure, locking both knees.

Hips should be level with the floor and rotated to L, with upper body facing the wall.

Note that photos illustrate the position at the end of Counts 2, 3 and 1.

38a

Extend both arms to the side at shoulder level, slightly forward and flexed, palms facing downward.

Keep fingers naturally relaxed throughout, shaping them optionally as described in Exercise 32.

38b

On Count &

Commence to move body forwards.

As LF passes RF, settle to R. Allow elbows to rotate inwards and palms to turn to face upward.

On Count 2

Check LF forwards, toe turned out, with only partial weight transfer.

Commence to move elbows forwards towards each other, keeping shoulders back and down.

> Downward Arm Movement (Exercise 34) with arms moving continuously and smoothly throughout.

38

38c

On Count &

Settle to L. At the same time begin to lower arms downwards.

On Count 3

Transfer almost full weight back to RF, retaining some pressure on toe of LF.

Continue to lower arms to pelvis level, palms facing inward.

38d

On Count &

As LF passes RF, settle to R. Rotate elbows outwards, palms turning to face towards body.

On Count 4-1

Place LF back for a Backward Walk, transferring weight gradually, using toe, ball then flat.

At the same time gradually and smoothly raise both arms from elbows almost to shoulder level and slightly forwards, with palms facing downward.

Keep shoulders down.

Continued overleaf

38 *Continued*

38e

On Count &

As RF passes the LF, settle to L and allow elbows to rotate inwards and palms to turn to face upward.

On Count 2

Place RF back for Last Backward Walk (as described in Exercise 14).

Commence to move elbows forwards towards each other, keeping shoulders back.

38f

On Count &

Settle to R and at the same time begin to lower arms downwards.

On Count 3

Transfer almost full weight to LF, retaining some pressure on toe of RF turned out.

Continue to lower arms to pelvis level, palms facing inward.

38g

On Count &

Settle to L. Rotate elbows outwards, palms turning to face towards body.

On Count 4-1

Place RF forwards for Forward Walk, transfering weight gradually.

At the same time gradually and smoothly continue to raise both arms from elbows almost to shoulder level and slightly forwards, with palms facing downward.

Keep shoulders down.

Repeat exercise using Counts or Rumba music.

Repeat exercise using both arms then one arm alternately with the other held horizontally palm down in the starting position.

Add up to 1/4 gradual body turn to L.

Repeat using Upward and Forward Arm Movement, as described in Exercise 35, both arms then one at a time alternating.

Optionally use Forward and Downward Arm Movement with the same Counts for forward and backward Cucarachas, both arms then one at a time alternating.

Alternatively, use Cha cha cha counting and music, replacing Rumba Forward Walk with Cha cha cha Lock Forward RLR and Rumba Backward Walk with Cha cha cha Lock Backward LRL.

Combination | Rumba Side Cucarachas with Arms

39

The purpose of the exercise is to develop the coordination between arm, body and leg movements as used, for example, in solo Side Cucarachas and Opening Out to L and R. The timing of the arm movement is >

Start in Rumba poise with feet apart, weight on LF and RF extended on toe with some pressure, both knees locked.

39a

Extend both arms to the side at shoulder level, slightly forward and flexed, with palms facing downward.

39b

On Count &

Settle to L and at the same time close RF to LF, RF on inside edge of ball with some pressure.

Allow L elbow to rotate inwards and palm to turn to face upward.

> different from that used for the Rumba Open Basic Movement in Exercise 38.

39c

On Counts 4 & 1

Transfer weight gradually onto RF inside edge of ball then flat, by straightening the R knee and releasing the heel of LF from the floor (as described in Exercise 6).

At the same time lower L elbow downwards in front of body to waist level, palm facing inward, with the arm in a shaped and gentle curve.

On Count &

Settle to R, allowing L knee to flex with LF on inside edge of ball with some pressure into the floor.

39d

On Count 2

Place LF to side with part weight, foot flat, and both knees straight.

Commence moving hips gradually from R neutral position level with the floor at the end of Count 2.

Start to bring the arm upwards through the elbow towards the side with the palm inward.

Continued overleaf

Continued

39e

On Count &

Transfer more (but not complete) weight onto LF and settle to L.

Keep knees locked, both feet flat.

Continue to extend L arm gradually through the elbow to the side, with palm facing downward.

39f

On Count 3

Transfer weight onto RF, foot still flat, allowing LF to rotate outwards onto toe with some pressure, with hips level to the floor and rotated to L.

At the same time complete extension of L arm to starting position.

Repeat exercise on RF and LF alternately using the arm movements as described.

Use Counts & 4 & 1 & 2 & 3 or Rumba music.

Optionally use the same Forward and Downward Arm Movement and timing in Hand to Hand steps.

More advanced dancers, use side body extension on Counts 1&, 2&, and connect with opposite hip and arm movement.

Rotation Exercises

Good turns are impressive and beautiful to watch. There are various kinds of turn in all Latin dances. They are created by storing and releasing energy through rotating different parts of the body with phased timings. It is therefore important to develop the ability to isolate the rotations of the different parts of the body and practice them. The first four exercises help to do this with the head, chest, pelvis and feet. Working at these exercises will also stretch the muscles in order to give greater flexibility and strength and so speed and sharpness. Isolated rotations are subsequently combined into turns with spotting and then settling action.

40

Head rotation is used in all kinds of Turn, with different degrees of rotation. Some, such as a full rotation of the body, require a large and quick movement of the head, and it is useful to stretch neck muscles and learn to control the movement.

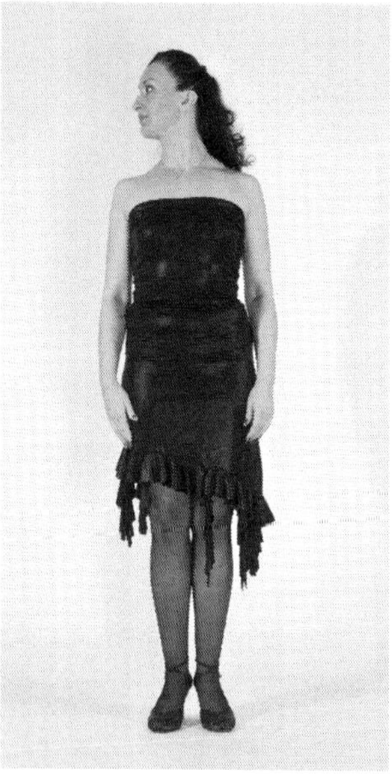

Start in general poise with feet together, knees slightly flexed, with arms hanging loosely at the side of the body.

Stretch the spine all the way through the neck to the crown of the head towards the ceiling, with eyes looking forward.

40a

On Count 1

Rotate the head from facing forward to R.

Keep the chin at a right angle to the neck, parallel to the floor, throughout.

Maintain the spine and neck in the starting position throughout.

On Count 2

Return to starting position.

40b

On Count 3

Rotate head from forward to L.

On Count 4

Return to starting position.

Continue exercise by rotating head to R and L.

Do slowly using Counts 1-4 or quick sharp rotations, using Counts 1,2.

Optionally use Rumba music for slow and soft rotations or Cha cha cha or Paso Doble music for sharp and quick rotations.

Chest rotation on its own is used extensively in Latin dance, for example, in leading Close Hip Twist and into the Fan in Rumba and Cha cha cha. The exercise helps to develop the chest rotating through the core's rotation and avoid the arms moving separately from the chest.

Start in general poise with feet together, knees slightly flexed.

Bring both arms in front of the body at shoulder level with palms of hands placed on insides of elbows.

Alternatively place hands on chest, forearms parallel to the floor.

41a

On Count 1

Rotate only the chest to R, focusing on rotating the core and maintaining arms in their starting position relative to the upper body.

Keep the pelvis facing forward without movement.

Keep the head still and facing forward.

On Count 2

Return to starting position.

41b

On Count 3

Rotate only the chest to L, focusing on rotating the core and maintaining arms in their starting position relative to the upper body.

On Count 4

Return to starting position.

Continue exercise by rotating chest to R and L.

Do slowly using Counts 1-4 or quick sharp rotations, using Counts 1,2.

Optionally use Rumba music for slow and soft rotations or Cha cha cha or Paso Doble music for sharp and quick rotations.

42

Pelvis rotation parallel to the floor is used extensively in many kinds of rotation and on its own in certain steps, for example in the small hip rotation before the Appel in Paso Doble.

Start in general poise with feet together, knees slightly flexed.

Raise arms to shoulder level parallel to floor, and place palms on top of each other facing downward.

Alternatively start with arm positions as described for Chest rotations (Exercise 41).

42a

On Count 1

Rotate only the pelvis towards R, keeping them level and parallel to the floor.

Ensure the head, chest and feet remain still.

On Count 2

Return to starting position.

42b

On Count 3

Rotate pelvis towards L.

On Count 4

Return to starting position.

Continue exercise by rotating pelvis to alternate sides using Counts 1–4, or to Cha cha cha or Paso Doble music for sharp and quick rotations or Rumba music for slow and soft rotations.

Rotate the pelvis alternately facing R and L, or facing R, Forward, L, Forward.

Lower leg rotation with foot twist is used extensively, but usually only in combination except for special choreography with twisting elements.

Start in general poise with feet together, knees slightly flexed.

Place both palms on the hips and press gently (this helps ensure that the hips stay level and still).

Transfer weight forwards onto balls of the feet, feet flat, to allow lower legs to rotate easily and feet to twist.

43a

On Count 1

Rotate both lower legs and twist feet towards R, on both feet flat, as much as possible without hip rotation.

Keep the head, upper part of the body and hips level and still.

On Count 2

Return to starting position.

43b

On Count 3

Repeat to L.

On Count 4

Return to starting position.

Ensure there is no rise and fall, with head remaining same height.

Continue exercise by rotating lower legs and twisting to R and L using Counts 1–4, or to Cha cha cha or Paso Doble music for sharp and quick rotations or Rumba music for slow and soft rotations.

Optionally repeat on

- *balls of feet*
- *heels of feet*
- *one foot flat, holding the other foot without weight in contact with the standing leg at ankle level.*

44

Full rotations that are sharp and balanced are always impressive to watch. This exercise combines the rotations of the different parts of the body >

Start in general poise with the feet together, slightly turned out, with arms hanging loosely at the sides of the body.

Find a spot at eye-level on wall or mirror (perhaps your own reflected eyes) on which to focus and to which the eyes will return following a sharp isolated rotation of the head before the body completes the turn.

44a

On Count 1

Start to rotate body to R.

Keep head still and the eyes spotting on the chosen fixed spot in the room. Pick up RF slightly and replace, foot flat with toe well turned out.

44b

On Count 2

Continue to rotate body to R, head still and eyes focussed on the same spot.

Allow the pelvis to continue rotate and as RF twists, close (or half close) LF to RF and change weight, foot flat.

> in Exercises 40-43 and adds the spotting action of the head and eyes to form effective full rotations.

44c

On Count 3

Continue to rotate body to R.

Pick up RF slightly and replace, foot flat with toe well turned out.

Now the head turns sharply to R to face starting direction and eyes focus on the same spot in the room.

Ensure that the neck and head remain perpendicular to the shoulders and floor.

44d

On Count 4

Allow body to turn underneath the stationary head as RF twists, close (or half close) LF to RF and change weight, foot flat.

Body completes full turn to R.

Repeat exercise several times to R and then to L.

Repeat varying the speed of the rotation, starting slowly and speeding up using counting:

- *1-8 with head rotation on 5*
- *1-6 with head rotation on 4*
- *1-4 with head rotation on 3 (as described above)*
- *1 & 2 with head rotation on the & (Spin Turn).*

Alternatively use Rumba or Cha cha cha or any Latin music.

45

To achieve sharp, precise and clear turns in Rumba and Cha cha cha, it is helpful to understand the principles of the movement and practice them. This exercise focuses on outward rotation as used in Checks From PP >

Start in Rumba poise and transfer almost full weight on RF towards ball and extend LF to side on toe with some pressure.

Both knees locked, hips central and level to the floor.

Extend arms to the side at shoulder level, slightly forward and flexed, with palms of the hands facing downward.

45a

On Count 1

Commence to rotate the upper part of the body from the waist up to R, keeping the head and feet still.

45b

On Count 2

Continue to rotate upper part of body to R and start to settle by moving and rotating hips slightly to R so that the body weight is now felt to be centre of RF.

The head and feet remain still in the same position.

The whole body is now rotated except for head and feet, which you can feel through the stretching of muscles in the neck, sides of the body and calves of the lower legs.

> and CPP (New Yorks), Spot Turns to R and L, Spin Turns and Swivels. The rotation begins with the upper body, then includes sides of the body, the hips with settling, and completes with feet and head.

45c

On Count 3

Continue the rotation still leading from the upper body.

Release this rotational energy by a strong twist on RF a $^1/_4$ turn to R.*

Ensure R knee stays locked throughout.

Close LF to RF without weight change on inside edge of ball with some pressure, with bent knee.

Turn the head sharply $^1/_4$ to R at the same time.

Complete settling by rotating hips R diagonally backwards, with body weight felt to be near the heel of RF.

45d

On Count 4

Recover to the starting position (facing in new direction) by bringing the hips central and level and extending LF to side on toe with some pressure.

Repeat the exercise on RF four times to complete a full turn to R.

Then repeat the same on LF turning to L.

Use Counts 1–4 or Rumba or Cha cha cha music.

**Also practice the exercise turning $^3/_8$, $^1/_2$, or, for advanced dancers, a full turn to R and L.*

46

To understand and improve inward rotation in Rumba and Cha cha cha, as used, for example, in Hand to Hand, Checks From PP and CPP (New Yorks). The rotation begins with the upper body, then includes the sides >

Start in general poise, taking almost full weight on RF and extending LF to side on toe with some pressure onto the floor.

Lock both knees with hips central and level.

Extend arms to the side at shoulder level, slightly forward and flexed, with palms of the hands facing downward.

46a

On Count 1

Commence to rotate the upper part of the body from the waist to L, keeping the head and feet still.

46b

On Count 2

Continue to rotate upper part of body to L and start to settle by moving hips diagonally forwards while rotating L. (This part of the hip movement is opposite to the usual one that is described in the previous exercise.)

Ensure knees remain locked.

The head and feet are still in the same position.

The whole body is now rotated except for head and feet, which you can feel through the stretching of muscles in the neck, sides of the body, thighs and calves.

> of the body, the hips with settling, and completes with feet and head. The difference to the previous exercise is rotation to L while on the RF (and conversely) and the hips starting to settle diagonally forwards before rotating diagonally backwards at the end of the rotation.

46c

On Count 3

Continue the rotation still leading from the upper body.

Release this rotational energy by a strong twist on RF a 1/4 turn to L.*

Ensure R knee stays locked throughout.

Close LF to RF without weight change on inside edge of ball with some pressure, with bent knee.

Turn the head sharply 1/4 to L at the same time.

Complete settling by rotating hips R diagonally backwards, with body weight felt to be near the heel of RF.

46d

Recover to the starting position (facing new direction) by bringing the hips central and level and extending LF to side on toe with some pressure.

Repeat the exercise on RF four times to complete the full turn to L.

Then repeat the same on the LF turning to R.

Use Counts 1–4 or Rumba or Cha cha cha music.

**Also practice the exercise turning 3/8, 1/2 or, for advanced dancers, a full turn to L and R*

Connection Exercises

Partner dances are formed of leaders and followers. The leader needs to be able to communicate the intended action to the follower through (usually) the hands as a result of body movement. This requires the right amount of matched tension in the arms and hands by each partner moving their body weight and axis to create and retain good connection and a common balance. This set of exercises helps develop the correct connection between two partners during different kinds of movement and handhold.

47 Push, neutral and pull

This exercise develops the feeling of push, neutral and pull through the forward and backward transfer of each body axis by each partner leaning their whole body line towards or away from the common couple centre. >

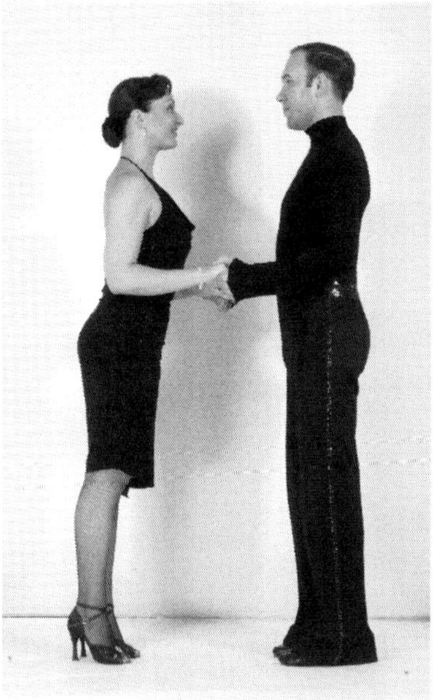

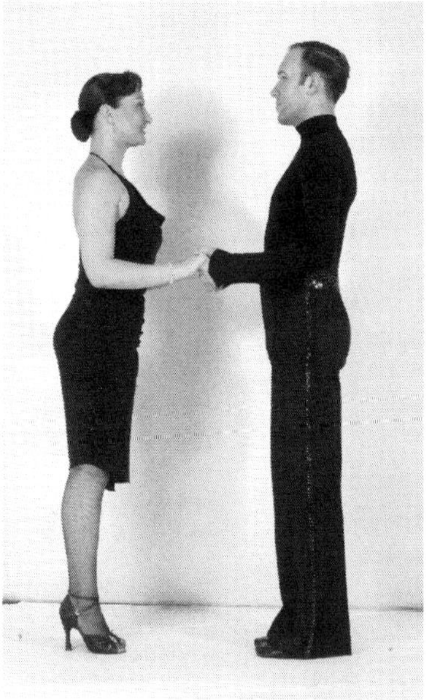

Start in general poise facing partner with feet together slightly turned out with weight equally distributed on both feet, kept flat throughout.

Take a double handhold at waist level with forearms facing straight forward.

47a

On Counts 1, 2

Both partners gradually transfer weight towards balls of feet moving the body axis forwards, ensuring each body moves as a whole leaning towards each other.

Feel how the tension gradually increases in the arms and hands as if pushing. Ensure elbows don't move behind the body and hands do not move to the side or outward.

47b

On Counts 3, 4

Both partners gradually transfer their weights onto the centre of both feet, returning to the starting position.

At the end of Count 4, attain a neutral position and feel how almost no tension is felt in the arms and hands.

> Movement is initiated by the leader, with the follower matching it equally in opposition in order to retain a common balance.

47c

On Counts 1, 2

Both partners gradually transfer weight towards the heels, moving the body axis backwards with body line leaning slightly backwards, keeping the spine straight.

Feel how the tension gradually changes in the arms and hands as if pulling.

Ensure fingers of both leader and follower retain good connection and do not extend, keeping elbows and wrists flexible.

47d

On Counts 3, 4

Gradually transfer weight forwards towards centre of both feet, returning to the starting position.

At the end of Count 4, attain neutral position and feel how almost no tension is felt in the arms and hands.

The hands are kept stationary throughout but there is a slight elastic movement backward and forward in the elbows and wrists.

Repeat exercise using a variety of speeds and handholds: Double (see photos), L to R, R to L, R to R and L to L, with different heights of waist, shoulder and eye level.

Use Counts or any Latin music.

48

The purpose of this exercise is to create the change in continuous tension in the arms ('Physical leading') as a result of the movement of the body >

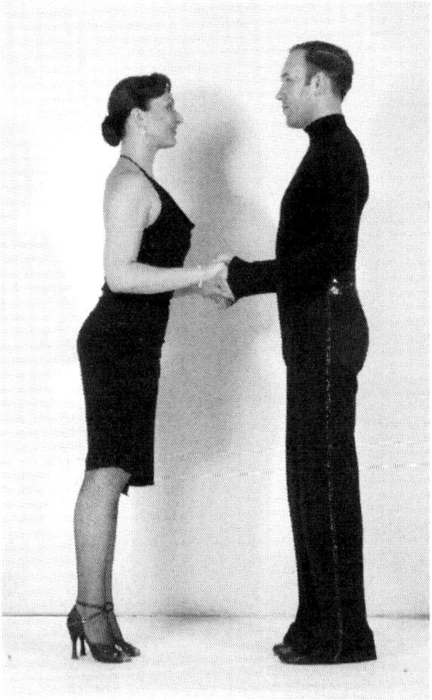

Start in general poise facing partner with feet together and toes slightly turned out, with knees straight but not locked.

Take a double handhold at waist level with forearms facing straight forward.

Transfer weight towards balls of feet.

Feel the tension in the arms gradually change as if pushing.

48a

On Count 1

Commence to transfer body axis and weight, leader to LF, follower to RF.

48b

On Count &

Leader settles to L and follower to R, with hips moving slightly to side and rotating diagonally backwards so that body weight is felt to be near the heels of standing legs.

Feel how the tension gradually changes in the arms and hands as if pulling.

> through weight change and settling which moves the body axes apart (rather than a change of lean in the body line as in the previous exercise).

48c

On Count 2

Commence to transfer body axis and weight, leader to RF, follower to LF.

Feel the gradual change in tension in the arms as if pushing.

The neutral position where almost no tension is felt in the arms and hands is felt at the ends of Counts 1 and 2.

48d

On Count &

Leader settles to R and follower to L.

Feel how the tension gradually changes in the arms and hands as if pulling.

The hands are kept stationary throughout, but there is a slight elastic movement backward and forward in the elbows and wrists.

Repeat exercise using a variety of speeds and handholds: Double (see photos), L to R, R to L, R to R and L to L, with different heights of waist, shoulder and eye level.

Use Counts 1 & 2 & 3 & 4 & or Rumba or Cha cha cha music.

49 The purpose of the exercise is to learn to lead and follow parallel and opposite body rotations, while maintaining appropriate tension and shape ('Shaping leading'). This will result in better connection in Underarm >

Start in general poise facing partner with double handhold at shoulder level, feet together (optionally with feet apart) and toes slightly turned out.

Transfer body weight towards balls of feet. Feel the change in tension in the arms like pushing.

49a

On Count 1

Leader initiates rotation of the upper part of body to L and follower reacts to L, keeping the arms almost in the same relative position and level.*

On Count 2

Continue to rotate, reaching the position where shape and balance can no longer be maintained.

The tension will be felt slightly more on the leader's front R hand.

49b

On Count 3

Leader initiates rotation to R and follow reacts by rotating to R.

On Count 4

Pass through the starting position.

Note: ensure the line of connection between the two partners does not change relative to the upper bodies.

> Turns in all Latin dances and also, for example, in the Rumba and Cha cha cha figures Alemana, Fan and Open Hip Twist, in the Samba Volte Spot Turns to R and L, and open PP, CPP and Fallaway positions in all dances.

49c

On Counts 5-6

Repeat rotation to R as described to L (Photo 49a).

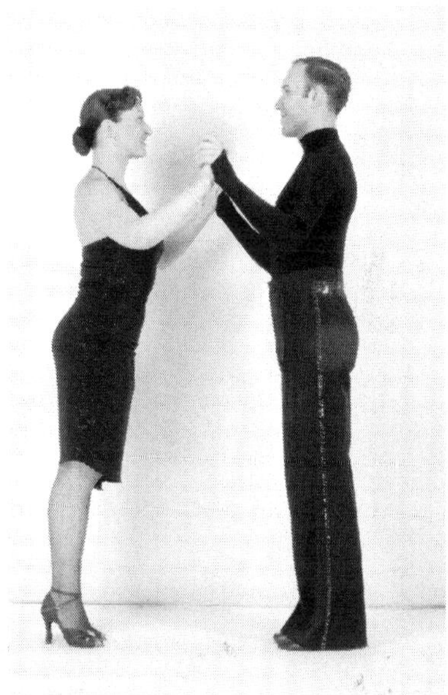

49d

On Count 7

Leader initiates rotation to L and follow reacts by rotating to L.

On Count 8

Pass through the starting position.

Notice that there is no position where almost no tension is felt in the arms and hands in this exercise.

Ensure that weight remains equally distributed on both feet throughout (avoid moving the body from one side to the other).

Repeat exercise using a variety of speeds and handholds: Double (as in photos), L to R, R to L, R to R and L to L, with different heights of waist, shoulder and eye level.

**Repeat using opposite rotation. This is where the leader rotates to L and follower to R, so that one side of the body is closer than the other. Leader initiates the difference by allowing the R elbow to flex more. The hands stay in the same line between the two partners.*

For advanced dancers, combine parallel and opposite rotation exercises with hip action as in previous Exercise 48.

Use Counts 1–8 as described or 1–4 or any Latin dance music.

50

There are many figures in Rumba and Cha cha cha where the leaders dance a Checked Forward Walk, transfering part weight, but allow followers to continue to move backwards and transfer their full weight, >

Stand in Rumba poise, facing partner with feet together, knees straight, and toes slightly turned out.

Take a double handhold at waist level with forearms facing straight forward.

Transfer weight towards balls of feet, moving body axis forwards.

50a

On Count &

Leader transfers almost full weight onto R leg and settles to R, follower to L.

Feel how the tension increases in the arms and hands as if pushing.

50b

On Count 2

Leader steps forwards with LF, with partial weight in Checked Forward Walk.

Follower steps RF back in Last Backward Walk, keeping the upper body forward for better poise and connection with the leader.

Feel the tension in the arms and hands gradually changes as if from pushing to neutral at the end of Count 2 where almost no tension is felt.

> for example, in Alemana from Open Position and Open Hip Twist. The purpose of this exercise is to learn how to maintain connection during this allowing movement ('Allowing leading').

50c

On Count &

Leader continues to transfer more weight on LF (no more than 70%), and settles to L.

By extending both elbows in a smooth elastic movement without locking, the leader allows the follower to complete Last Backward Walk.

Feel how the tension in arms and hands gradually changes from neutral to feeling like pulling at the end of Count &.

50d

On Count 3

Both transfer weight in place. Knees locked, hips level to the floor.

Feel how the tension in the arms and hands gradually changes as if pulling to neutral at the end of Count 3.

On Count &

Complete weight transference, both settling (see Photo 50a).

Feel how the tension in the arms and hands gradually changes from neutral to feeling like pushing at the end of Count &.

Repeat exercise using a variety of speeds and handholds: Double (see photos), L to R, R to L, R to R and L to L, with different heights of waist, shoulder and eye level or Close Hold.
Use Counts as described or Rumba or Cha cha cha music.

Notes